MAKING BIG WORDS

Multilevel, Hands-On Spelling and Phonics Activities

by
Patricia M. Cunningham
and Dorothy P. Hall

illustrated by Tom Heggie

Cover photo by Dennis Fraise

ISBN No. 0-86653-807-0

Printing No. 191817

Good Apple
A Division of Frank Schaffer Publications
23740 Hawthorne Blvd.
Torrance, CA 90505

DEDICATION

For Our Children–David, Suzanne, and Michelle

A special thanks to
Rosalyn Morgan, photographer,
and April Corn, teacher–
both '92 graduates of Wake Forest University's
Elementary Education Program–
and to the children at
Clemmons Elementary School, Winston-Salem, N. C.,
who starred in the photos

TABLE OF CONTENTS

LESSONS INDEX (IN ALPHABETICAL ORDER)

G1499

51. girlfriend ed ing ide ind....52
girl ride find fire file fine fined fired filed/field fiend grind glide firing filing finger linger friend infield grinder fielding girlfriend

52. graduation tion a (ago/again) ug....53
go ago out dug rug ran run ruin tuna again round around ground guitar during ration outran aground adoring radiant duration graduation

53. grandmother ed other road-rode roam-Rome....54
arm road rode Rome roam moan groan grand armed other anger hanger danger manger ranger magnet dragon moaned mother another grandmother

54. grasshopper pro ph ess op....55
pop hop hops/shop hero grass graph press phase phrase gopher proper prosper oppress perhaps progress grasshopper

55. hamburgers g ag ug age ush (bush, brush)....56
us as gas/sag rag rug hug huge rage sage Mars bush mush brush Amber ambush hamburgers

56. headquarters er/est qu est....57
hard head rest rude ruder ahead squad squat quart quest rudest square harder hardest quarter request headset headrest treasure headquarters

57. helicopters s/es ch th sh itch their-there....58
***A two-day lesson or pick and choose!**
chop port hero echo itch ship this these those their there/three pitch porch torch choir cheer sheer shirt elect select itches echoes heroes heroic hotels polite police pitcher pitches porches torches reptile respect shelter ostrich heliport helicopters

58. hospitals sh it ot ip op....59
sip hip hop hot hit sit spit spot/stop shop shot ship slip split pilots/pistol polish hospitals

59. hurricanes er air are hare-hair....60
air hair hare care/race cash racer ranch chair China share scare nurse curse search rancher cashier hurricanes

60. imagination tion a(ago) ain an in....61
in an go ago tin tan man main gain again among giant nation ignition maintain animation imagination

61. impossible ile imp iss ess oss oil....62
imp oil soil boil limp mile boss loss moss miss mess less bless bliss blimp smile spoil mobile missile possible impossible

62. incredible ible in er ine ind end....62
end lend dine line bind blind blend diner liner cider edible binder lender blender decline recline inedible credible incredible

63. indestructible in ible er/est er ide ense....63
***A two-day lesson or pick and choose!**
send nice ride side cute cuter nicer build dense tense bride cutest nicest edible direct secure bruise cruise sender tender insure insult inside insider include slender builder/rebuild license disturb dentist dentures district distinct interest indirect insecure inedible credible incredible distribute indestructible

76. marshmallows all ash ow 70
who/how row mow low all mall wall hall show slow Mars rash mash smash small allow alarm aroma solar worms marshal marshmallows

77. Massachusetts s/es sh th ch ash 71
hut huts/shut that chat math mash cash much such each teach/cheat chest match attach mashes cashes matches attaches mustache Massachusetts

78. measurements ment sure ture en er 71
eat use user/sure amuse smart steam eater eaten nature mature assure steamer smarten measure amusement measurements

79. microphones c/ch ph imp ice..72
ice imp rich echo crimp chimp chomp choir price porch pooch phone chrome copier enrich prince phonics phonier morphine microphones

80. microscopes com im pro ope 72
pro prom pose rope cope mope press comic scope impose impress promise process compose composer compress microscopes

81. millionaire ain ane oan one miner-minor main-mane loan-lone..73
name/mane lane main rain mine moan loan lone alone miner minor lemon/melon remain normal airline mineral million millionaire

82. mischievous mis ome ouse some-sum 74
use sum some come home hiss miss mess moss muss shoes house mouse movie music voice misuse mischievous

83. motorcycles ly y er ose...75
room cost sore/rose rosy loot lose loser close motor storm roomy cycle cycler stormy sorely costly looter motorcycles

84. mountains uni ain ount 76
man main unit must mast mist most moist minus stain/saint mount amount suntan unions/unison mansion mountain mountains

85. multiplication tion ic al ill amp ump ount maul-mall 77
***A two-day lesson or pick and choose!**
all ill pill mill mall maul Paul atom lamp lump clump clamp count mount limit local total panic attic topic atomic amount action auction/caution caption tuition lunatic Titanic million capitol mutation complain complaint municipal political politician limitation multiplication

86. mysterious ous y-messy y-ies 78
try tour mess rust rose rosy rusty messy moist tries story storm stormy stories serious tourism moisture mysterious

87. neighborhoods ed ing ood ore idge..78
be boo good hood bore sore shore snore booed bored being/begin brood ridge bridge booing boring ignore behind songbird neighbor neighborhoods

88. operation tion er pane-pain rain-rein 79
pane pain rain rein riot/trio ratio patio paint point option/potion portion painter pointer operation

89. outstanding un and ant io-audio, studio 80
do out ant and sand undo said soda auto audio stand giant donut unsaid suntan studio distant instant astounding outstanding

90. parachutes ture ear 80
up set ear hear tear pear spear shear upset earth search chutes capture pasture pushcart parachutes

91. perfectly re ly ee 81
fee free tree flee rely left type fleet creep crept repel reply lefty elect freely celery retype reflect perfect perfectly

92. performances per re ace ance 81
ran cap open face once fence force space peace reran recap refer reopen person menace prance perform enforce romance performances

93. permission/impression im sion en or-ore 82
or ore more sore/rose rise ripe ripen risen snore press person prison sermon impose impress mission emission imprison impression/permission

94. personality per le/el/al ist eal 82
real teal steal petal panel spine spinal spiral triple person tinsel pastel spaniel apostle realist parents pertain panelist ponytail personal personality

95. pickpockets ick ock oke et it 83
pet pit sit set kick pick tick sick sock coke poke spoke stick stock socket pocket picket cockpit pickpockets

96. playground y a-aloud ay ound oud 83
dry pry pay pray play ugly your loud proud young angry pound round aloud along dragon around ground aground laundry playground

97. Popsicles™ ip op ice ose 84
ice pop cop sip lip lips/slip clip slop plop pose close slice spice splice police copies Popsicles™

98. population tion an in ot ip op 84
in pin tin tan pan pot/top pop pit/tip lip lot not plan plop plot pilot tulip lotion potion/option optional population

99. porcupines ine urse ure sun-son 85
sun son sure pure cure pine spine curse purse nurse super supper person prison copper copier cousin insure precious porcupines

100. president pre ent ie tied-tide 85
pie die tie tied/tide rent dent sent spent resent serpent/present pretend preside pretends resident president

101. quarterbacks qu ack uck et 86
bet set sack rack back buck truck stuck stack track quack quart struck bucket racket basket bracket setback quarter backrest barracks quarterbacks

102. rattlesnake re er/est kn ale 86
late/tale sale lean knee kneel knelt later snake reset resale retest relate rattle latest leaner leanest anteater rattlesnake

103. responsibility y y-ies re less oss 87
***A two-day lesson or pick and choose!**
try spy oil oily only less loss boss type poet pony pity rely reply style tries spies noise noisy bossy story point resist ponies poetry pointer noisily stories stepson pitiless oiliness possible pointless possibility responsibility

117. superintendent en (entire/deepen) un pre ed ipe....................................96
***A two-day lesson or pick and choose!**
pin tie tied seen teen pest stun deep ripe ripen super enter endure entire pinned untied unseen deepen pester intend stripe striped preteen pretend present stunned interest nineteen unpinned pestered interested presented president turpentine uninterested superintendent

118. superstitious ess est ort 96
tour rest test pest port sort sport press issue tissue tiptoe stress resist pursue pursuit tourist serious protest posture superstitious

119. telephones e ee ope ost 97
he she see stop/spot/pots/post host lost hope slope elope these those sleep slept tepee hotel honest steeple telephones

120. television sion in ent..97
vest vent sent vote/veto even event novel visit inlet invite invest vision silent/listen violin violet violent novelist novelties television

121. temperature pre ture er eat meet-meat 98
eat meat meet treat trump temper tamper repeat mature mutter trumpet pretreat repeater tamperer mutterer trumpeter premature temperature

122. Thanksgiving kn ight ing ang ink ank night-knight.......................98
ink sink sing sang gang knit thank think thing sting stink stank sight night knight vanish sinking thinking vanishing Thanksgiving

123. thermometers re th et other 99
set met them theme teeth other reset meter meteor retest remote mother mothers/smother/thermos restore remorse thermometers

124. thoughtless less out ost ut..99
out hut gut shut/huts guts/gust lost host ghost guest guess outlet outset shuttle gutless thought thoughtless

125. thunderstorm ue ern umor do-due..100
umor-humor, rumor, tumor do-due
do due Sue true humor tumor rumor storm stern south north detour modern student monster thunder southern thunderstorm

126. touchdowns ow (cow,show) own (down,shown) to-too-two........................100
do to too two/tow cow how now/own undo show snow town down shown touch outdo shutdown touchdowns

127. transportation tion ot int...101
pot spot/stop pint print sprint sprain strain potato parrot nation notion potion portion station patriot airport nonstop transport transportation

128. traveling al/le/el ail tail-tale..101
rent vine tale tail trail/trial rival tiger giant angle/angel travel gravel rental tangle tingle native vinegar triangle traveling

MAKING BIG WORDS AND CONNECTIONS ACROSS THE CURRICULUM

To be effective, phonics and spelling instruction should be tied as closely to what children are reading and learning about as possible. In selecting the word that ends the lesson, we have included many words which teachers may use as part of their themes or units. Here are some of the curriculum connections possible from the words in this book.

Family/Community: neighborhoods apartments grandmother

Foods/Nutrition: applesauce breakfast chocolates hamburgers marshmallows Popsicles™ sandwiches spaghetti strawberries vegetables watermelon

Transportation: airplanes transportation traveling helicopters

Sports: basketball autographs championship quarterbacks wrestling

Animals: grasshopper birdhouse chimpanzee jellyfish porcupines rattlesnake woodpeckers

Science: circulation conservation atmosphere earthquakes hurricanes mountains experiments microscopes satellites temperature weightlessness

Social Studies: Massachusetts communities constitution continents democratic generations international president revolution Thanksgiving Washington

Mathematics: subtraction multiplication measurements

Describing Words: astonishing comfortable frightening impossible incredible indestructible irresponsible mischievous mysterious outstanding resourceful ridiculous superstitious thoughtless unbelievable uncomfortable undependable unforgettable wonderful

MAKING BIG WORDS–THEORY AND RESEARCH

Making Big Words is an activity in which students are individually given some letters and use these letters to make words. During the fifteen- to twenty-minute activity, students make approximately fifteen to twenty words, beginning with short words and continuing with bigger words until the final word is made. The final word always includes all the letters they have that day, and students are usually eager to figure out what word can be made from all these letters. Making Big Words is an active, hands-on, manipulative activity in which students discover letter-sound relationships and learn how to look for patterns in words. They also learn that changing just one letter or even just the sequence of the letters changes the whole word (Cunningham, 1991; Cunningham & Cunningham, 1992).

After making the words, the students help the teacher to sort the words for patterns. They may pull out all the words that begin alike or that have a particular spelling pattern or vowel sound. They also sort for endings, prefixes and suffixes, homophones (close, clothes), and compound words.

Making Big Words is a multilevel activity because, within one instructional format, there are endless possibilities for discovering how our alphabetic system works. By beginning every Making-Big-Words activity with some short, easy words and ending with a big word that uses all the letters, the lessons provide practice for the slowest learners and challenge for all. It is a quick, every-pupil-response, manipulative activity with which students get actively involved.

Spelling pattern and word family instruction has a long history in American reading instruction. Currently, research from several areas supports the long-standing practice of word family/phonogram/spelling pattern instruction. The research of Treiman (1985) suggests that both students and adults find it much easier to divide syllables into their onsets (all the letters before a vowel) and rimes (vowel and what follows) than into any other units. Thus *Sam* is more easily divided into *S-am* than into *Sa-m* or *S-a-m*. It is easier and quicker for people to change *Sam* to *ham* and *jam* than it is to change *Sam* to *sat* and *sad*. In fact Treiman concludes that the division of words into onset and rime is a "psychological reality." Wylie and Durrell (1970) listed thirty-seven phonograms which could be found in almost five hundred primary grade words. These high-utility phonograms are:

> **ack, ail, ain, ake, ale, ame, an, ank, ap, ash, at, ate, aw, ay, eat, ell, est, ice, ick, ide, ight, ill, in, ine, ing, ink, ip, it, ock, oke, op, ore, ot, uck, ug, ump, unk.**

Another area of research supporting spelling patterns is the research conducted on decoding by analogy (Goswami & Bryant, 1990). This research suggests that once students have some words which they can read and spell, they use these known words to figure out unknown words. A reader confronting the infrequent word *flounce* for the first time might access the known words *ounce* and *pounce* and then use these words to generate a probable pronunciation for *flounce*.

Brain research provides a different sort of support for word family instruction. Current theory suggests that the brain is a pattern detector, not a rule applier, and that decoding a word occurs when the brain recognizes a familiar spelling pattern or, if the pattern itself is not familiar, searches through its store of words with similar patterns (Adams, 1990). To decode the unfamiliar word *knob*, for example, the child who knew many words that began with *kn* would immediately assign to the *kn* the "n" sound. The initial *kn* would be stored in the brain as a spelling pattern. If the child knew only a few other words with *kn* and hadn't read these words very often, that child would probably not have *kn* as a known spelling pattern and thus would have to do a quick search for known words which began with *kn*. If the child found the words *know* and *knew* and then tried this same sound on the unknown word *knob*, that child would have used the analogy strategy. Likewise, the child might know the pronunciation for *ob* because of having correctly read so many words containing the *ob* spelling pattern or might have had to access some words with *ob* to use them to come up with the pronunciation. The child who had no stored spelling patterns for *kn* or *ob* and no known words to access and compare to would be unlikely to successfully pronounce the unknown word *knob*.

Big words have some additional patterns beyond the common one-syllable spelling patterns. The patterns in big words include prefixes and suffixes which give semantic clues about meanings for words in addition to serving as pronunciation chunks. Recognizing the prefix *mis* in words like *misread* and *mistreat* helps students access both meaning and pronunciation. In *Mississippi* and *mistletoe,* the *mis* still helps with pronunciation but not with meaning. Suffixes such as *tion* and *al* affect the pronunciation of words and change where in the sentence the words can be used. In English, many big words are just little words with added prefixes and suffixes. (When you act in a certain way, you perform an action. Sometimes an action provokes a reaction. People who overreact are called reactionaries.)

To determine how good readers decode and spell big words, we must consider what we know about how the brain functions and specifically how big words are analyzed and divided. Decades of research by Mewhort and colleagues (summarized in Mewhort & Campbell, 1981 and in Adams, 1990) demonstrate that good readers "chunk" or divide big words into manageable units. They do this based on the brain's incredible knowledge of which letters usually go together in words. If you did not recognize the word *midnight* in print, you would divide it as you saw it, between the *d* and the *n*. For the word *Madrid,* however, you would divide after the *a,* leaving the *dr* together. Interletter frequency theory explains this neatly by pointing out that the letters *dr* often occur together in syllables in words you know (drop, dry, Dracula). Words with the letters *dn* in the same syllable are almost nonexistent. (This also explains why beginners might pronounce *f-a-t-h-e-r* as "fat her," but children who have some words from which the brain can generate interletter frequencies will leave the *th* together and pronounce "father.")

Psychological theory suggests that the brain functions as a pattern detector. Successfully decoding a word occurs when the brain recognizes a familiar spelling pattern or, if the pattern itself is not familiar, searches through its store of words with similar patterns. To find patterns in big words, the brain "chunks" the word not based on rules but on its incredible knowledge of interletter frequencies. Once big words are chunked, readers use patterns from known big words to decode the unfamiliar words. In order to use patterns from known words, readers must have a store of multisyllabic words which they can read and spell.

If you ask the students what they think of Making Big Words, they will probably answer, "It's fun!" From the moment they get their letters, they begin moving them around and making whatever words they can. They are particularly eager to figure out the word that can be made with all the letters. Once the students begin making the words the teacher asks them to make, the activity is fast-paced and keeps the students involved. They also enjoy the sorting. Students put words together in groups that have the same spelling pattern, prefix, suffix, or other pattern, and then other students have to guess why they put those particular words together. Making-Big-Words lessons involve the students in looking at words and manipulating words. Through these activities, they learn to recognize and spell many big words, and they discover the patterns that allow them to decode and spell new big words.

REFERENCES

Adams, M. J. *Beginning to Read: Thinking and Learning About Print.* Cambridge, MA: MIT Press, 1990.

Cunningham, P. M. *Phonics They Use: Words for Reading and Writing.* New York: HarperCollins, 1991.

Cunningham, P. M., & J. W. Cunningham. "Making Words: Enhancing the Invented Spelling-Decoding Connection." *The Reading Teacher,* (1992), 46, 106-115.

Goswami, U., & P. Bryant. *Phonological Skills and Learning to Read.* East Sussex, U.K.: Erlbaum Associates, 1990.

Mewhort, D. J. K., & A. J. Campbell. "Toward a Model of Skilled Reading: An Analysis of Performance in Tachistoscoptic Tasks." In G. E. MacKinnon & T. G. Walker (Eds.), *Reading Research: Advances in Theory and Practice,* (1981), vol. 3, 39-118. NY: Academic Press.

Trieman, R. "Onsets and Rimes as Units of Spoken Syllables: Evidence from Children." *Journal of Experimental Child Psychology,* (1985), 39, 161-181.

Wylie, R. E., & D. D. Durrell. "Teaching Vowels Through Phonograms." *Elementary English,* (1970), 47, 787-791.

PREPARING AND TEACHING A MAKING-BIG-WORDS LESSON

Picture 1: The teacher has decided that *motorcycles* is the big word that will end the lesson. She has written *motorcycles* on an index card. Here she is brainstorming lots of words that can be made from the letters in *motorcycles*.

Picture 2: The teacher has decided which of the many words that could be made will best illustrate some spelling patterns. She writes these words on large index cards.

Photos by Rosalyn D. Morgan

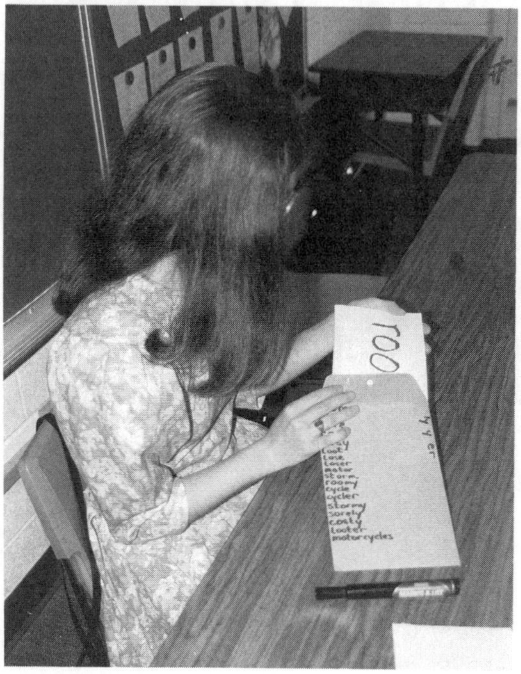

Picture 3: She puts the large index cards on which she has written the words in a small brown envelope. On the outside of the envelope, she writes the words in the order the students will make them and the patterns for which she will have them sort.

Picture 4: The children are given strips containing the letters of the big word. For *motorcycles*, their strip has the printed letters *e o o c c l m r s t y*, vowels and then consonants in alphabetical order so as not to give away what the big word is. The children cut the strips into individual letters. They then have two minutes to figure out all the words they can make from these letters before making the words the teacher has decided they should make.

Photos by Rosalyn D. Morgan

Picture 5: Here are the words the teacher had the children make from the letters in *motorcycles*. After the children made each word, the teacher put the index card in the pocket chart. They will use these words to sort for patterns.

Picture 6: After all the words are made, the teacher and children sort for various patterns. Here a student has pulled out *room, roomy* and *storm, stormy*. He will also pull out *rose, rosy*. The teacher and students will talk about how adding the *y* changes where in the sentence you can use the word and point out the spelling change in *rose-rosy*.

Photos by Rosalyn D. Morgan

HOW TO USE THIS BOOK

The Making-Big-Words lessons in this book have been used by many teachers. Teachers pick, choose, and adapt the lessons to suit the needs of their own classes. The lessons are ordered alphabetically by the big word that ends the lesson but can be done in any order. The index at the back indicates which letter patterns are sorted for in each lesson. Some teachers teach several lessons in a row which have a particular pattern students need practice with.

Each Making-Big-Words lesson is multilevel in two ways. The students begin by making some simple, short words and then make more complex, long words. The sorting is also multilevel in that students sort for phonograms, endings, prefixes, suffixes, compound words, and homophones. Since most classrooms contain students at all different stages of spelling/decoding ability, making easier and more difficult words and sorting for easier and more difficult patterns allow all students to increase their word knowledge.

Most lessons can be done in fifteen to twenty minutes, with approximately two-thirds of the time spent making big words. The other one-third of the time is spent sorting words for patterns and transferring this word knowledge to spelling a few new words. Some lessons are so rich in possibilities for word making and pattern sorting that they are designated as two-day lessons. If the lesson seems too long, you could omit certain words and/or patterns. With these longer lessons, many teachers like to make all the words on one day and then sort all the words the following day.

In teaching the lessons, you may want to omit certain words and add others. You may not want to sort for all the patterns or to sort for patterns not suggested. But, to keep the lesson multilevel, you will want to include words and patterns on a variety of levels. Some teachers worry that the least able students will not be able to make the long words and that the advanced students do not need to make the short words. Observations of these lessons indicate that if they are fast-paced, most students stay involved. Even if some students don't get every letter of a big word in place before the word is placed in the pocket chart, they usually get some of the letters and then finish the word by matching to the model. Advanced students enjoy seeing how many different words they can make in the initial two minutes of the lesson and are eager to figure out the big word that can be made with all the letters.

In addition to the lessons and the index, this book contains reproducible letter strips. Some teachers duplicate enough strips so that each student can take home an uncut strip of the letters used in the lesson. Students can't wait to take the strips home and say, "I bet you don't know the big word that can be made when you use all these letters!" At home they cut the strips into letters and let someone–parent, brother, sister, grandmother–try to make the big word. They then proudly demonstrate words they can remember making and how they sorted these words into patterns.

Making Big Words is a manipulative, multilevel activity which both teachers and students enjoy. As they make and sort words, the students increase their word knowledge, discover patterns, and become more able readers and writers.

PLANNING YOUR OWN MAKING-BIG-WORDS LESSONS

Once you get started making big words, you will find that many of the words which tie into your content are not included in our lessons. It is fun and easy to plan lessons of your own. Here are the steps we went through to plan our lessons.

1. Decide what the final word in the lesson will be. In choosing this word, consider student interest, what curriculum tie-ins you can make, and what patterns you can draw students' attention to through the word sorting at the end.
2. Make a list of words that can be made from the letters of the final word.
3. From all the words you listed, pick approximately fifteen to twenty words that include the following:
   a. Words that you can sort for the pattern(s) you want to emphasize
   b. Little words and big words so that the lesson is multilevel
   c. Words that can be made with the same letters in different places (anger/range) so students are reminded that when spelling words, the order of the letters is crucial
   d. Words that most of the students have in their listening vocabularies
   e. Homophones and compound words
4. Write all the words on index cards and order them from smallest to biggest.
5. Order them further so that you can emphasize letter patterns and how changing the position of the letters or changing/adding just one letter results in a different word.
6. Store the cards in an envelope. Write on the envelope the words in order and the patterns you will sort for at the end.

STEPS IN TEACHING A MAKING-BIG-WORDS LESSON

1. Have someone pass out letter strips and have each student cut the strip into individual letters.

2. Give the students two minutes to write down as many words as they can that can be made from their letters. They should move the letters around to make a word, write this word on a piece of scrap paper, and then make another word. They can use a letter twice only if they have two of that letter. Some teachers let students work with a partner during this initial two minutes.

3. When the two minutes are up, quickly go around the room and let students tell and spell one word they made. Tell students that there are hundreds of words that can be made from these letters and that they made some wonderful words.

4. Tell students that you have some particular words you want them to make in a particular order so that they can see how words change as just a letter or two are changed. Tell them that some of the words you will ask them to make are probably words they figured out and made on their own.

5. Hold the index card with the first word in the lesson so that the students cannot see the word. Tell them the word and how many letters they will need to make it. "Take four letters and spell *room*." Watch as the children make *room* and then call on a child who has *room* made correctly to spell *room* for everyone. Put the index card on which *room* is written in the pocket chart. Encourage anyone who has not spelled *room* correctly to fix it.

6. Continue having them make words in the order you decided. Use the words in simple sentences if necessary to access meaning. Cue them as to whether they are just changing one letter, changing letters around, or moving all their letters to make a word from scratch. Tell them how many letters they will need for each word.

7. As each word is made, call on someone who you see has spelled the word correctly to spell it for everyone. Put that word in the pocket chart and encourage anyone whose spelling is incorrect to fix the word.

8. Before telling them the last word ask, "Has anyone figured out what word we can make with all our letters?" If so, congratulate those students, and have them make it with their letters. If not, say something like, "I love it when I can stump you. Use all your letters and make *motorcycles*."

   Some teachers make the words on one day and then do Steps Nine and Ten the following day.

9. Once all the words have been made, have students say and spell the words in the pocket chart with you. Use these words for sorting and pointing out patterns. Pick a word and point out a particular spelling pattern and ask students to find the others with that same pattern. Group these words in the pocket chart so that the pattern is visible.

10. To get maximum transfer to reading and writing, have them use the patterns they have sorted to spell a few new words that you say.

A STEP-BY-STEP TOUR THROUGH A MAKING-BIG-WORDS LESSON

The students have their strips containing the letters *e o o c c l m r s t y*.

They cut the strip into letters and have two minutes in which to manipulate the letters and make as many words as possible, writing these on a piece of scrap paper. When the two minutes are up, the teacher lets each student tell and spell one of the words made. The teacher congratulates the students on all the wonderful words they made and then tells them that they are going to make some particular words in a particular order so that they will have words to sort for particular patterns.

The teacher then begins the part of the lesson in which students make words selected by the teacher.

Take four letters and make *room*.

Let's make another four-letter word, *cost*.

Here is another four-letter word, *sore*. (When you break your arm, it is very sore.)

Now use the same four letters you used in *sore*, but change them around and make the word *rose*.

Change just the last letter and you can turn *rose* into *rosy*.

Now make a new four-letter word, *loot*. (During a riot people sometimes loot things from stores.)

Let's make one more four-letter word, *lose*.

Add one letter to *lose* to make the five-letter word *loser*.

Make the five-letter word, *close*. (This *close* is the word that we use when we ask someone to close the door.)

Make another word that takes five letters, *motor*.

Take five letters and make *storm*.

You have made *room* already; use five letters and spell *roomy*.

The last five-letter word we will make today is *cycle*. (We have been learning about the water cycle.)

We are now going to six-letter words. If you add just one letter to *cycle*, you will have a *cycler*. (Sometimes we call the person who rides a bicycle a cycler.)

You made the word *storm*; take six letters and spell *stormy*.

You made the four-letter word *sore*; add two letters and make the six-letter word *sorely*. (When the secretary was absent, she was sorely needed.)

Let's make another word that ends in *ly*, *costly*.

Our last six-letter word is *looter*. (A person who loots is a looter.)

Now, we come to the last word, the big word that can be made with all the letters. Has anyone figured it out? (If so, congratulate those students and have them make it. If not, tell them to arrange all their letters and spell *motorcycles*.)

When the students have made *motorcycle*s, draw their attention to the words they made; have them read the words with you; and help them sort for a variety of patterns: *room, cost, sore, rose, rosy, loot, lose, loser, close, motor, storm, roomy, cycle, cycler, stormy, sorely, costly, looter, motorcycles.*

Find the words that end is *ose–rose, close, lose.*

Point out the different pronunciations for the spelling pattern *ose* and the two pronunciations and meanings for *close.*

Usually *o-s-e* is pronounced as we pronounce it in *rose* and *close.* Spelling patterns sometimes have other pronunciations, and you hear the other pronunciation for *o-s-e* in the word *lose.* There is also another pronunciation for *close,* as in this sentence: Don't get too close to the fire!

Find the pairs that end in *y–room, roomy; storm, stormy; rose, rosy.*

When the students have found the pairs, use the words in sentences to show how the words are related and how we use them in different places in the sentences.

> A room that is big is roomy.
>
> When we have a storm, we say it is a stormy day.
>
> Something that is pink or sweet like a rose is rosy.

Next, find the pairs that end in *ly–sore, sorely; cost, costly.*

When the students have found the pairs, use the words in sentences to show how the words are related and how we use them in different places in the sentences.

> *Sore* sometimes means painful. When we say people were sorely missed or sorely needed, we mean they were painfully missed or needed.
>
> Something that costs a lot is costly.

Let's find the *er* pairs–*lose, loser; loot, looter; cycle, cycler.*

> Sometimes *er* means the person or thing that does something. What does a loser do? A looter? A cycler?

Once the sorting is done, point out the spelling changes that occur in *rose, rosy; lose, loser; cycle, cycler.*

What if you were writing and you needed to spell *chose*? Which words would help you spell *chose*? What if you were writing and needed to spell *closely*? Which of the endings we sorted for would help you spell *closely*?

1.

LETTERS:  a e e u d n r s t v

WORDS TO MAKE:

at	rat	near	tuner	tender
	sat	dear	enter	nature
	ear	deer		venture
		nest		dearest
		rest		nearest
		vest		dentures
		dune		**adventures**
		tune		

SORT FOR: ture at est dear-deer tune-tuner

Pull out all the *est* words–*nest, rest, vest, dearest, nearest*–and help students to notice how *est* is pronounced the same in all the words. Then put *dearest* and *nearest* next to *dear* and *near* and show how these endings change the words.

WRITING AND NEED TO SPELL:

pest (-est)
tenderest (-est)

2.

LETTERS:  a e e e i d m n r s t t v

A two-day lesson or pick and choose some words.
You may want to make all words one day and sort and spell the next day.

WORDS TO MAKE:

art	date	risen	driven	neatest
arm	mean	eaten	marine	meanest
eat/	neat	state	artist	smarten
ate	read	smart	desire	sardine
	mine	admit	admire	dentist
	dine	treat	advise	deserve
	vine	drive	disarm	distant
	rise		inmate	misread
			insert	mistreat
			meaner	advertise
			neater	determine
				terminate
				interested
				advertisement

SORT FOR: ad de in mis dis ist en-eaten
er/est ate ine-dine, sardine, determine

Pull out all the *ine* words; then separate them and note the three different pronunciations for *ine*. For the prefixes and suffixes, point out that sometimes they give you clues to meaning–an artist is a person who creates art–but sometimes they are just pronunciation chunks–a dentist is not a person who creates dents!

WRITING AND NEED TO SPELL:

skate (-ate)
misadvertised (mis-)
disinterested (dis-)

3.

LETTERS:  a a e i l n p r s

WORDS TO MAKE:

air	pair	plain	praise
	pear	plane	spaniel
	pail	learn	**airplanes**
	pale	arena	
	sale	alien	
	sail	raise	
	sane		
	lane		
	pane		
	pain		
	rain		

SORT FOR: ain ane ale ail pair-pear pane-pain plane-plain pail-pale sale-sail

Help students to notice that the pairs *ale/ail* and *ane/ain* usually have the same pronunciation. When you want to spell a word that rhymes with them, you have to see if it "looks right" or check a dictionary.

WRITING AND NEED TO SPELL:

brain (-ain)
snail (-ail)

Help students to realize that *brain* could be *b-r-a-n-e* and that *snail* could be *s-n-a-l-e*. Write them both ways and let them decide which "looks right." Let one student look them up in the dictionary just to be sure.

4.

LETTERS:  a a a e i b c h l l p t

WORDS TO MAKE:

cap
tap
lap

clap
itch
able

cable
table
batch
latch
patch
pitch
petal
label

chapel
palace
capital
capable
alphabet
alphabetical

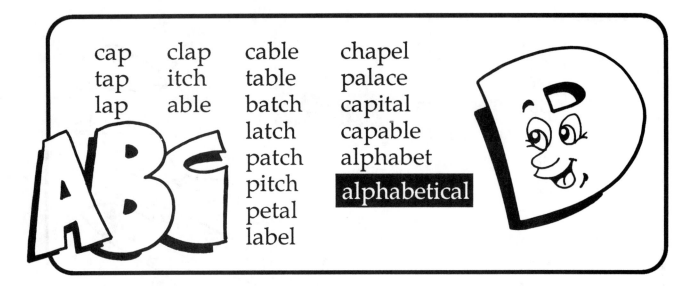

SORT FOR: el/le/al ap atch itch able
alphabet-alphabetical

Have the students find all the words that end in *el, le,* and *al.* Help them to notice that these endings are all pronounced similarly. Tell them that when spelling a word that ends with this sound, you cannot be sure which way it will be spelled. You have to write it and see if it "looks right" or check it in a dictionary.

WRITING AND NEED TO SPELL:

catch (-atch)
switch (-itch)

5.

LETTERS:  a a e m n p r s t t

WORDS TO MAKE:

The / means that the next word can be made just by changing where the letters are. It is important that students learn that spelling requires not only that all the letters be there but that they be in the right places. Cue them when they will use the same letters in a different order to spell a new word.

ear	near	arena	stream
	tear	apart	matter
	pear	spear	spatter
	team/	smear	pattern
	tame	stamp	**apartments**
	same	tramp	
	ramp	steam	
	area		

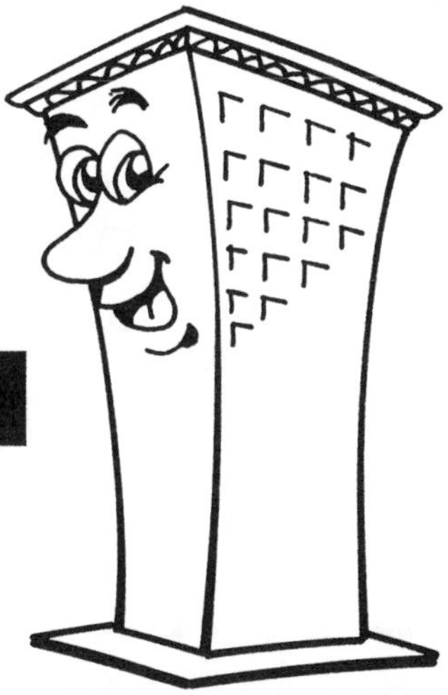

SORT FOR: a (apart/area) ame amp eam ear atter

Pull out all the *ear* words–*ear, near, tear, pear, spear, smear*–and help students notice the two different pronunications commonly given to *ear*. Point out also that *tear* has two different pronunciations–you tear paper and you see a tear rolling down someone's cheek. Help students to notice that the *a* at the beginning and end of *arena* has the same sound and to listen for this sound at the beginning of *apart* and *apartments* and at the end of *area*.

WRITING AND NEED TO SPELL:

cream (-eam)
cramp (-amp)

6.

LETTERS:  a a e e u c l p p s

WORDS TO MAKE:

The / means that the next word can be made just by changing where the letters are. It is important that students learn that spelling requires not only that all the letters be there but that they be in the right places. Cue them when they will use the same letters in a different order to spell a new word.

ape	slap	place	escape
cap	clap	space	asleep
lap	cape	sauce/	appeal
	lace	cause	capsule
		pause	applause
		apple	applesauce
		sleep	

SORT FOR: ause ace ap ape

Include all the words with a particular chunk–*cause, pause, applause, ape, cape, escape*–and help students to notice that many chunks have the same sound at the end of short and longer words. Point out the *sleep-asleep* morphemic relationship.

WRITING AND NEED TO SPELL:

because (-ause)
scrape (-ape)

7.

LETTERS:  a e u g m n r s t

WORDS TO MAKE:

The / means that the next word can be made just by changing where the letters are. It is important that students learn that spelling requires not only that all the letters be there but that they be in the right places. Cue students they will use the same letters in a different order to spell a new word.

use/	germ	surge	nature
Sue	game	argue	mature
gum/	tame	amuse	magnet
mug	true	anger/	urgent
rug	menu	range	strange
gem	urge		mustang
			arguments

SORT FOR: ture g (gum-gem) ame ange ug ue use urge-urgent argue-arguments

Pull out all the words which have a *g*. Then separate them into *gum* and *gem* columns. Help students to notice that the *gem* sound is usually the sound you hear when *g* is followed by *e–anger* being the exception. Help them recognize the *urge-urgent, argue-arguments* morphemic relationships.

WRITING AND NEED TO SPELL:

refuse (-use)
future (-ture)

8.

LETTERS:  a i i o g h n n s s t

WORDS TO MAKE:

The / means that the next word can be made just by changing where the letters are. It is important that students learn that spelling requires not only that all the letters be there but that they be in the right places. Cue students when they will use the same letters in a different order to spell a new word.

at	hit	gash	gnash	insist	nothing	astonish
it	hat	hang	stash	assign		astonishing
	sat	sang	sting			
	sit	song	thing			
	ash	sing/				
		sign				
		gnat				

SORT FOR: ash it at ang ing gn
sang-song-sing sit-sat

Pull out all the *ing* words and help students to notice that *ing* is an ending on *astonishing* but just a spelling pattern in the other words. Point out the *thing-nothing* morphemic relationship. Help them notice that the *gn* has the same sound at the beginning of *gnat* and *gnash* and at the ending of sign and assign.

WRITING AND NEED TO SPELL:

swing (-ing)
splash (-ash)

9.

LETTERS:  a e e o h m p r s t

WORDS TO MAKE:

map	heat	shape	preheat
tap	hear	reset	reshape
sap	here	phase	hamster
set	trap	phrase	atmosphere
		sphere	
		reheat	
		repeat	
		remote	
		stereo	
		preset	

SORT FOR: pre re ph ap hear-here sphere-atmosphere

Pull out all the *re* and *pre* words and help students see that sometimes *re* and *pre* change the meaning of the word, and sometimes they are just pronunciation chunks. When you *reheat, reshape,* or *reset* something, you heat it or shape it or set it again, but when you *repeat,* you don't peat again! Students should learn that prefixes and suffixes sometimes give them meaning clues and almost always help them pronounce big words.

WRITING AND NEED TO SPELL:

prefer (pre-)
pretest (pre-)

10.

LETTERS:  a a o u g h p r s t

WORDS TO MAKE:

hug	hour	group	sought	autographs
rug	sour	sport	author	
our	auto	spurt	graphs	
	part	apart		
	port	sugar		
	sort	tough		
	hurt	rough		
	soup	ought		

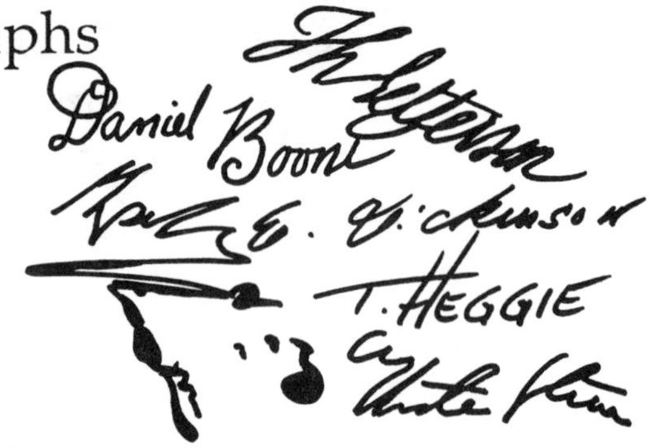

SORT FOR: ug ought ough oup urt ort
our-hour graphs-autographs

WRITING AND NEED TO SPELL:

short (-ort)
bought (-ought)

If *short* and *bought* rhyme in your dialect (or in the dialect of your students), have them spell more distinct words, perhaps *slug* and *blurt*.

11.

LETTERS:  a a e b b k l l s t

WORDS TO MAKE:

bat	tall	least	basket
bet	ball	beast/	basketball
let	bell	baste	
all	tell	stall	
	sell	blast	
	last		
	best		
	east		

SORT FOR: all ell et ast east

WRITING AND NEED TO SPELL: feast (-east) swell (-ell)

12.

LETTERS: e i o u b d h r s

WORDS TO MAKE:

bus/	side	brush	bruise	rosebud
sub	hide	bride		hideous
rub	bird	shrub		birdhouse
	rose	shred		
	hose	horse		
	bush	house		
	rush			

SORT FOR: ub ush ide ose

Pull out all the *ush* words and then have students notice the two different pronunciations for this spelling pattern.

WRITING AND NEED TO SPELL: push (-ush) crush (-ush)

13.

LETTERS:  e i o b d f n r y

WORDS TO MAKE:

Ed	red	fine	drone
	bed	dine	forbid
	Ned	done	beyond
	boy	bone	friend
	one	bond	**boyfriend**
		fond	
		Fred	
		obey	

SORT FOR: ed ine ond one

Pull out all the *one* words and then help students sort them according to the two common pronunciations for this spelling pattern.

WRITING AND NEED TO SPELL:

stone (-one)
pond (-ond)

14.

LETTERS: a a e b f k r s t

The / means that the next word can be made just by changing where the letters are. It is important that students learn that spelling requires not only that all the letters be there but that they be in the right places. Cue students when they will use the same letters in a different order to spell a new word.

WORDS TO MAKE:

ask	task	baker	streak/
	fast	skate	skater
	take	break/	karate
	fake	brake	basket
	bake	stake/	**breakfast**
		steak	
		freak	

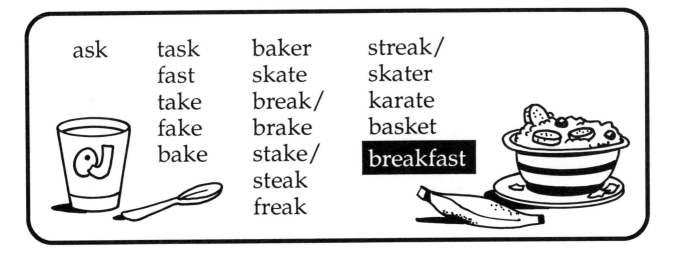

SORT FOR: er eak ake ask break-brake steak-stake

Pull out all the *eak* words and then separate them into two columns according to the two common pronunciations for this spelling pattern. Help students to notice that *eak* and *ake* are often pronounced the same way. If you need to spell a word that rhymes with *break/brake,* you have to write it to see if it looks right or check it in the dictionary. Point out the *bake-baker, skate-skater* morphemic relationship.

WRITING AND NEED TO SPELL:

mask (-ask)
sneak (-eak)

15.

LETTERS:  e i b g h n r s s t

The / means that the next word can be made just by changing where the letters are. It is important that students learn that spelling requires not only that all the letters be there but that they be in the right places. Cue students when they will use the same letters in a different order to spell a new word.

WORDS TO MAKE:

big	sign	risen	bright	brighten
bin	sigh	birth	signer/	rightness
tin	rise	night	resign	brightness
sin		sight	bigness	
		right		

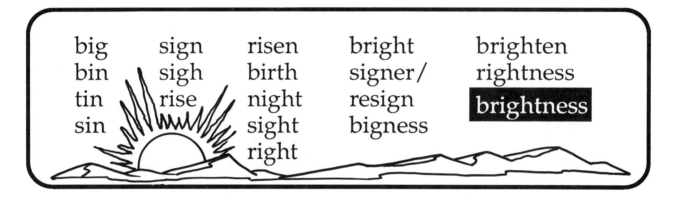

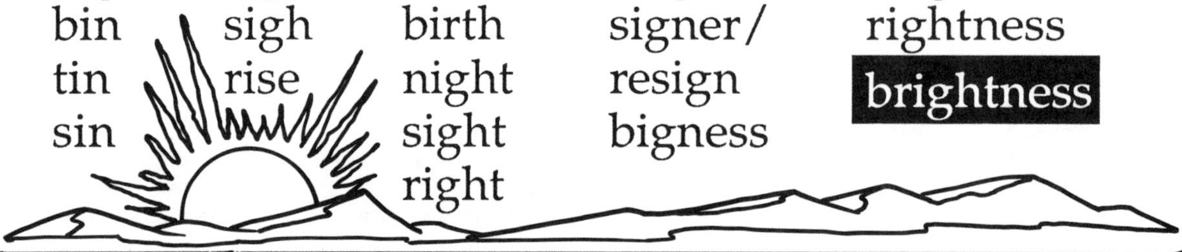

SORT FOR: ness en (risen, brighten)
in ight

WRITING AND NEED TO SPELL:

tight (-ight)
tighten (-en)
tightness (-ness)

16.

LETTERS:  a e e i o b c l n r t

A two-day lesson or pick and choose some words.
You may want to make all words one day and sort/spell the next day.

WORDS TO MAKE:

cat/	brain	trance	certain	clarinet
act	train	center	toenail	bracelet
ice	elect	cereal	earlobe	relation
rice	react/	relate	trainee	election
nice	crate	rebate	cabinet	reaction
rain	cabin	locate		relocate
late	lance	notice		liberate
cent		action		reliance
				tolerance
				celebration

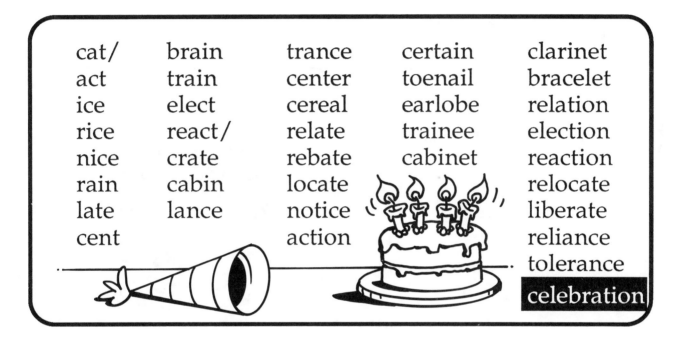

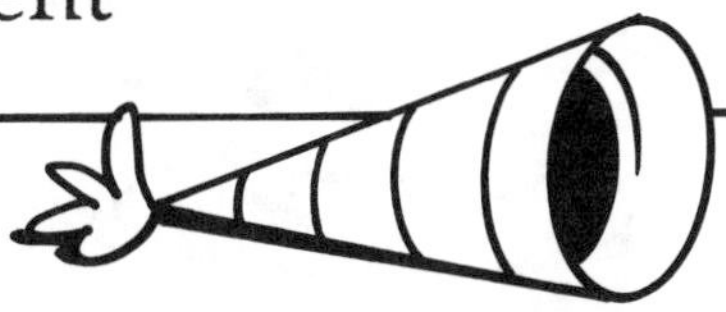

SORT FOR: re tion c (cat/cent) ate ain ice ance

Pull out all the *re* words; then separate those that change the meaning of the word and those that are just pronunciation chunks. When you regain something, you gain it back. The *re* on *relate* helps you with pronunciation but not meaning. Divide the c words into *cat/cent* columns and notice that the words in the *cent* column all have the letter *e* following the *c*.

WRITING AND NEED TO SPELL:

mice (-ice)
retrain (re-)
location (-tion)

17.

LETTERS:  a i i o c h h m n p p s

The / means that the next word can be made just by changing where the letters are. It is important that students learn that spelling requires not only that all the letters be there but that they be in the right places. Cue them when they will use the same letters in a different order to spell a new word. Remind students that countries' names begin with a capital letter as you ask them to make *China*.

WORDS TO MAKE:

sip	ship	smash	spinach
hip	shop	pinch	champions
hop	chop	champ	championship
	chip	China	
	chin/	panic	
	inch	chaos	
	cash	mocha	
	mash		

SORT FOR: sh ch inch ip op ash
champ-champions-championship

Pull out all the *ch* words, then divide them into *chop/chaos* columns and help the students notice that *ch* usually has the sound you hear in *chop* but sometimes has the sound in *chaos–Christmas* being the most common example.

WRITING AND NEED TO SPELL:

trip (-ip)
crash (-ash)

18.

LETTERS:  a e e i c h m n p z

The / means that the next word can be made just by changing where the letters are. It is important that students learn that spelling requires not only that all the letters be there but that they be in the right places. Cue them when they will use the same letters in a different order to spell a new word. Remind them that a country's name begins with a capital letter as you ask them to make *China*. Give students a sentence for *impeach* if you think they might not know the meaning of this word.

WORDS TO MAKE:

cap	mice	peach	menace
ace	inch/	pinch	cinema
ice	chin	China	impeach
	pace	champ	machine
	camp	chimp	mechanize
	ache/	cheap	chimpanzee
	each	cheep	

SORT FOR: c/ch-all five sounds   each   ace
cheep-cheap

All words have the letter *c* and can be divided into five columns headed by *cap, ice, inch, ache,* and *machine. Machine* is the the only word here which has this uncommon sound. Help the students to notice that in words in which *c* has the sound in *ace, c* is followed by the letter *e* or *i*.

WRITING AND NEED TO SPELL:

teach (-each)
space (-ace)

19.
LETTERS: 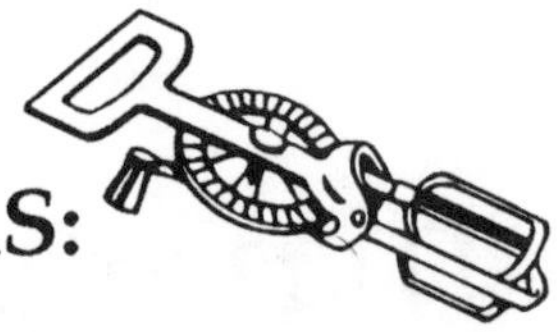 i u c h k m n p s

WORDS TO MAKE:

Ump is short for *umpire*. You may need to give students a sentence to build meaning for the words *chump* and *spunk*.

ump	pink	chump	punish
ink	mink	chunk	chipmunks
	sink	spunk	
	sunk	punch	
	hunk	munch	
	sick	music	
	pick		
	Nick		
	hump		

SORT FOR: ick ink unk unch ump

WRITING AND NEED TO SPELL: lunch (-unch) stink (-ink)

20.
LETTERS:  a e o o c c h l s t

WORDS TO MAKE:

cool	catch	choose	locates
tool	latch	closet	catches
ache	coach	castle	coaches
echo	teach	school	clothes
	tools	locate	chocolates
	chase		
	close		
	chose		

SORT FOR: c-ch s/es ool atch
close-clothes choose-chose

Note the two sounds for *ch* as in *ache* and *coach*. Help the students to notice that *es* is added when the word ends in *ch*. Also note the two pronunciations and different meanings for the word *close*.

WRITING AND NEED TO SPELL: pools (-ool, s) matches (-atch, es)

21.

LETTERS:  a i i o u c c l n r t

The / means that the next word can be made just by changing where the letters are. It is important that students learn that spelling requires not only that all the letters be there but that they be in the right places. Cue them when they will use the same letters in a different order to spell a new word. Remind students that a name begins with a capital letter as you ask them to make *Carl*. Give them a sentence for *lunatic* if you think they might not know the meaning of this word.

WORDS TO MAKE:

cat/	cart	carton	auction/
act	Carl	arctic	caution
art/	count	critic	lunatic
tar		clinic	narcotic
car		action	circulation

SORT FOR: tion ic ar art

WRITING AND NEED TO SPELL:

star (-ar)
smart (-art)

22.

LETTERS:  a a i o o u b c h l p r s t

A two-day lesson or pick and choose some words.
You may want to make all words one day and sort/spell the next day.

WORDS TO MAKE:

sub/	bush	pouch	rascal	capital
bus	push	brush	slouch	capitol
	cost	crush	phobia	plastic
	lost	pilot	phobic	robotic
	host	robot	author	haircut
	post	polar	cohost	sailboat
	ouch	photo	postal	subpolar
			public	tropical
			tropic	coauthor
			copilot	acrophobia
				subtropical
				claustrophobia

SORT FOR: ic al co sub ph ouch
ost (cost-host) ush (bush-brush)
capital-capitol

According to Webster, *capital* means a letter and the place where your state government can be found; *capitol* is the building in which your government meets! Pull out all the *ic* and *al* words; then separate those that change the meaning of the word and those that are just pronunciation chunks. A person with a phobia is phobic, and *robotic* refers to what robots do. The *ic* on the end of *plastic, public,* and *tropic* is a pronunciation chunk but not a meaning chunk. Likewise, the *al* on *postal, tropical,* and *subtropical* is a meaning chunk, but the *al* on the end of *rascal* is just a pronunciation chunk.

WRITING AND NEED TO SPELL:

crouch (-ouch)
hush (-ush)

23.

LETTERS:  a e o o b c f l m r t

The / means that the next word can be made just by changing where the letters are. It is important that students learn that spelling requires not only that all the letters be there but that they be in the right places. Cue students when they will use the same letters in a different order to spell a new word.

WORDS TO MAKE:

ace	able	cobra	marble
	foot	combo	combat
	bear/	coral	comfort
	bare	metal	barefoot
	race	camel	footrace
	cola	motel	**comfortable**
	coma		

SORT FOR: com el/le/al ace bear-bare

Have the students find all the words that end in *el, le,* and *al*. Help them to notice that these endings are all pronounced similarly. Tell them that when you are spelling a word that ends with this sound, you cannot be sure which way it will be spelled. You have to write it and see if it "looks right" or check it in a dictionary. Also point out the different pronunciations for *com*.

WRITING AND NEED TO SPELL:

place (-ace)
hotel (-el)

G1499

24.

LETTERS:  a e i o c c l m m r s

WORDS TO MAKE:

aim	maim	claim	comics	comical
	came	camel	circle	miracle
	same	coral	soccer	calories
	lame	comma	social	memorial
				commercials

SORT FOR: com el/le/al ame aim

Have the students find all the words that end in *el, le,* and *al.* Help them to notice that these endings are all pronounced similarly. Tell them that when you are spelling a word that ends with this sound, you cannot be sure which way it will be spelled. You have to write it and see if it "looks right" or check it in a dictionary. Point out that the spelling patterns *ame* and *aim* are usually pronounced the same. Also point out the different pronunciations for *com.*

WRITING AND NEED TO SPELL:

flame (-ame)
shame (-ame)

Have students write the words both possible ways–*flaim, flame; shaim, shame.* Decide which ones look right, and check their choices in the dictionary.

25.
LETTERS:  e i i o u c m m n s t

WORDS TO MAKE:

cut	cute	noise	income	comment
	mute	comet	insect	commute
	into		cities	counties
	menu		cousin	communist
	nose		minutes	communities
			commits	

SORT FOR: com in s/es ute

Note the two pronunciations for *com*. Write *city, county,* and *community* on the board, and help students to see that when a word ends in *y*, you change the *y* to *i* and then add *es*.

WRITING AND NEED TO SPELL: flute (-ute) compute (com-, -ute)

26.
LETTERS:  e o u c m p r s t

WORDS TO MAKE:

cut	cute	crust	custom
	mute	mouse	costume
	rust	super	compute
	must		customer
	most		computers
	post		
	cost		
	poem		
	poet		

SORT FOR: ute ust ost (cost/most)
poet-poem

Pull out all the *ost* words and then have students notice the two different pronunciations for this spelling pattern.

WRITING AND NEED TO SPELL: frost (-ost) trust (-ust)

27.

LETTERS:  a e i o o c n n r s t v

A two-day lesson or pick and choose some words.
You may want to make all words one day and sort/spell the next day.

WORDS TO MAKE:

act	ocean/	cannot	cartoon	ancestor
ice	canoe	nation	contain	overcoat
rice	actor	native	consent	overcast
nice	react	active	convert	reaction
noon		action	connive	investor
soon		notice	tension	inventor
		novice	version	contrive
		insect	erosion	conversion
		invent	evasion	conversation/
		invest	ancient	**conservation**
		strive		
		carton		

SORT FOR: con sion tion or oon ice ive

Note the two pronunciations for *con*. Also note that *tion* and *sion* have the same pronunciation. Pull out all the *ice* and *ive* words, and note the two different pronunciations for these chunks. Help students to realize that the *or* at the end sometimes indicates a person. Point out morphemic relationships between words including *ancient* and *ancestor*.

WRITING AND NEED TO SPELL:

pension (-sion)
invention (-tion)

28.

LETTERS:  i i o o u c n n s t t t

WORDS TO MAKE:

in	soon	cotton	suction
inn	noon	cousin	tuition
out	noun	notion	instinct
sun	count		**constitution**
son	scout		
	snout		
	union		
	onion		

SORT FOR: tion oon out inn-in sun-son

WRITING AND NEED TO SPELL:

trout (-out)
motion (-tion)
baboon (-oon)

29.

LETTERS:  i o o u c c n n r s t t

WORDS TO MAKE:

out	scout	unison	constrict
tour	snout	unicorn	construct
unit	trout	coconut	**construction**
	onion	tourist	
	union	contour	

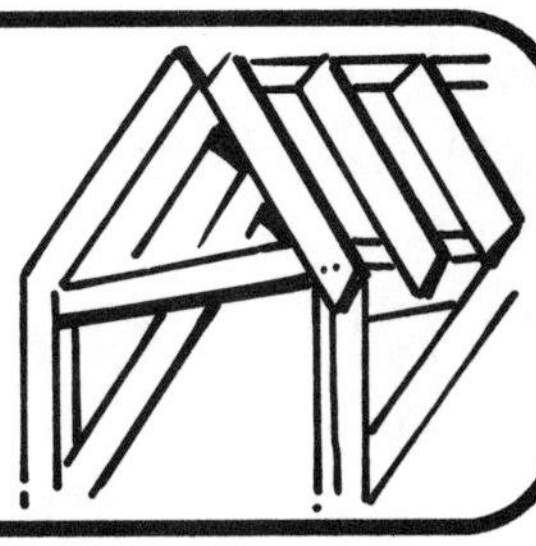

SORT FOR: con uni out onion-union

Help students realize that a unicorn has one horn and that when you sing in unison, it sounds as if one voice is singing. The prefix *uni* often means one or the same.

WRITING AND NEED TO SPELL:

trout (-out)
motion (-tion)
baboon (-oon)

30.

LETTERS:  e i o c n n n s t t

The / means that the next word can be made just by changing where the letters are. It is important that students learn that spelling requires not only that all the letters be there but that they be in the right places. Cue students when they will use the same letters in a different order to spell a new word. Cue them to the meanings for *sent, cent,* and *scent* before they make these words.

WORDS TO MAKE:

one	scent	contest
none	stone	consent
tone	insect	contents
cone/	tennis	innocent
once	notice	**continents**
sent		
cent		

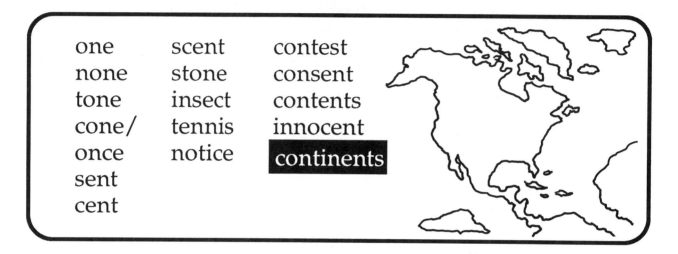

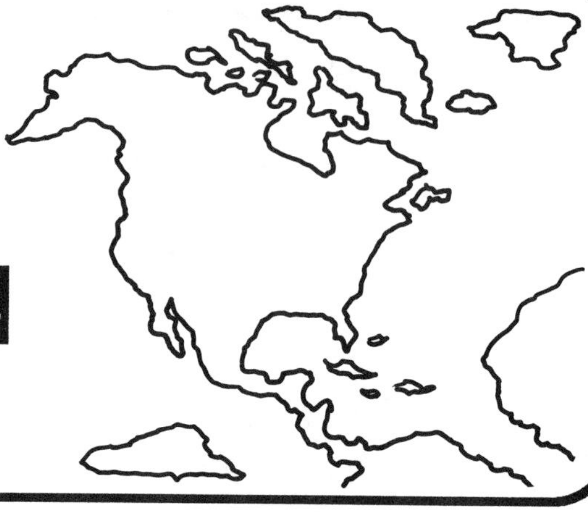

SORT FOR: con one ent sent-cent-scent

Pull out all the *one* words and then help students sort them according to the two common pronunciations for this spelling pattern.

WRITING AND NEED TO SPELL:

spent (-ent)
condone (con-, -one)

31.

LETTERS: 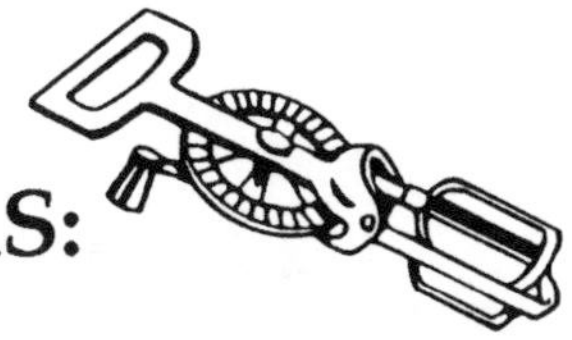 e e i o b c l n r t v

WORDS TO MAKE:

rice	broil	relive	recline	violence
coin	elect	recent	convert	contrive
coil	rebel	recite	violent	election
		recoil		**convertible**
		loiter		

SORT FOR: con re c/c oil

Note the different pronunciations and meanings for the *re* chunk. To relive is to live again. When you recoil, you draw back and when you recline, you lie back. Help students see morphemic relationships including *violent, violence* and *convert, convertible.*

WRITING AND NEED TO SPELL: spoil (-oil) confuse (con-)

32.

LETTERS: 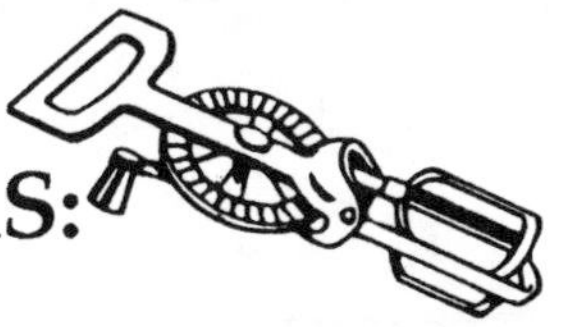 a o c k l r s s s w

WORDS TO MAKE:

cow	claw	cross
low	slaw	Carol
law	slow	slacks
	crow	across
	sock	**crosswalks**
	lock	
	rock	
	rack	
	sack	
	walk	

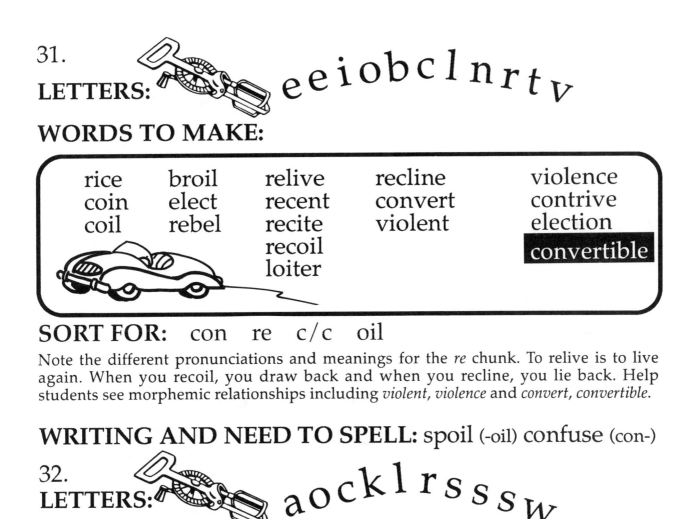

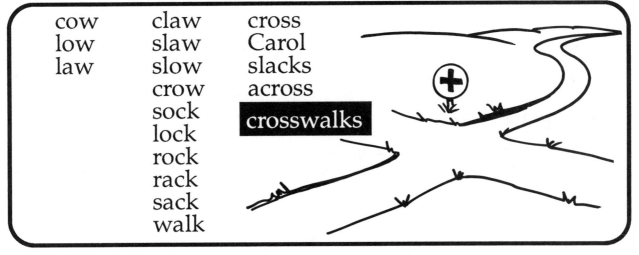

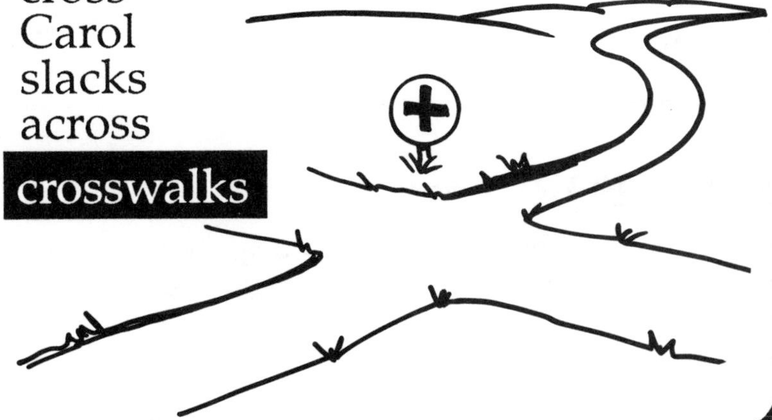

SORT FOR: aw ack ock ow

Note the different pronunciations for *ow.*

WRITING AND NEED TO SPELL: throw (-ow) straw (-aw)

33.

LETTERS:  a e i o c c d m r t

The / means that the next word can be made just by changing where the letters are. It is important that students learn that spelling requires not only that all the letters be there but that they be in the right places. Cue them when they will use the same letters in a different order to spell a new word. Cue students to the meanings for *made* and *maid* before they make these words.

WORDS TO MAKE:

die
diet/
tide
time
dime
made
maid
atom
idea
coma

comet
comic
crime
timer
medic

metric
atomic
democrat
democratic

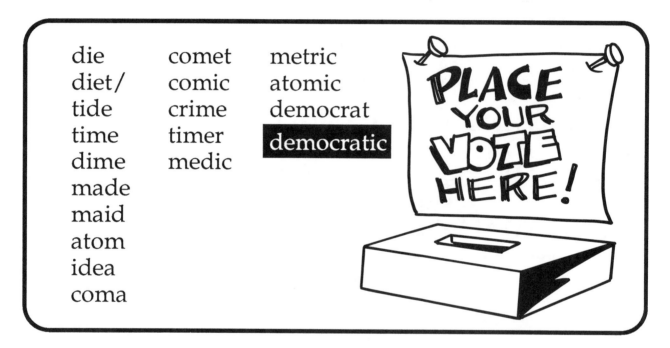

SORT FOR: com ic ime made-maid

Pull out out all the *com* words and help students notice the two different pronunciations. Point out morphemic relationships including *time, timer; atom, atomic;* and *democrat, democratic.*

WRITING AND NEED TO SPELL:

grime (-ime)
public (-ic)

34.

LETTERS:  a i i o c d n r t y

The / means that the next word can be made just by changing where the letters are. It is important that students learn that spelling requires not only that all the letters be there but that they be in the right places. Cue students when they will use the same letters in a different order to spell a new word.

WORDS TO MAKE:

day	dirt	corny	action
Ray	rain	candy	ration
act	tray	dairy/	carton
cry	corn	diary	crayon
dry		dirty	dictionary
		rainy	
		radio	
		ratio	
		actor	

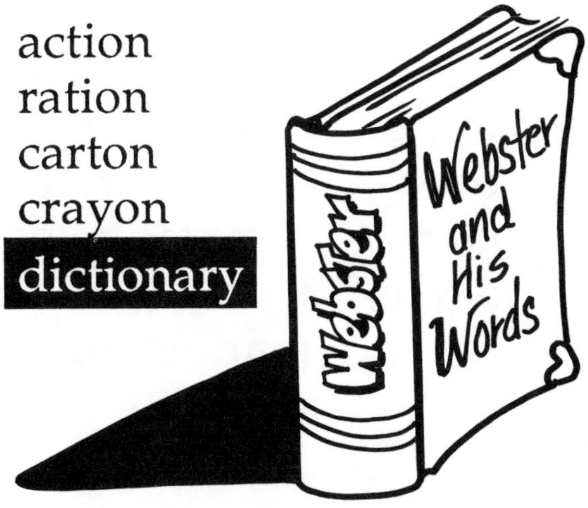

SORT FOR: tion y ay act-actor-action radio-ratio

Help students notice the two different pronunciations for *y* and that sometimes *y* signals a morphemic relationship as in *dirt, dirty; rain, rainy.* Be sure to have students notice the *tion* in the middle of *dictionary*. Point out the *io* that both *radio* and *ratio* end with.

WRITING AND NEED TO SPELL:

spry (-y)
spray (-ay)

35.

LETTERS:  a e e e i d g m n r s s t

A two-day lesson or pick and choose some words.
You may want to make all words one day and sort/spell the next day.

WORDS TO MAKE:

mad	admire	sardine	disaster	messenger
arm	assign	derange	disagree	eagerness
tame	resign	message	demerits	readiness
mine	design	segment	tameness	greediness
dine	detain	migrate	sediment	agreements
sign	disarm	migrant	regiment	disagreements
agree/	merits	madness	determine	
eager	marine	disease	designate	
admit			teenagers	

SORT FOR: de dis ad ment ness ine ign

Note the two pronunciations for *de*. Also note that *tion* and *sion* have the same pronunciation. Pull out all the *ine* words and note the three different pronunciations as in *mine, marine,* and *determine*. Write *ready* and *greedy* on the board and help students notice that the *y* changes to *i* when *ness* is added. Point out morphemic relationships between words.

WRITING AND NEED TO SPELL:

decline (de-, -ine)
define (de-,-ine)

36.

LETTERS:  a a a e e i c d n p p r s

WORDS TO MAKE:

Tell students the meaning intended before having them make *peace, piece.*

paid	apiece	spender
raid	prance	disappear
space	appear	sandpaper
spade	arcade	appearance
spend	parade	disappearance
paper	dipper	
dance	spider	
peace		
piece		

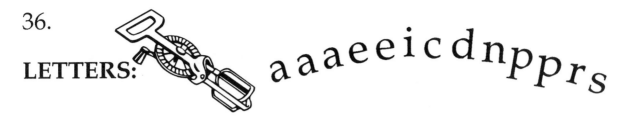

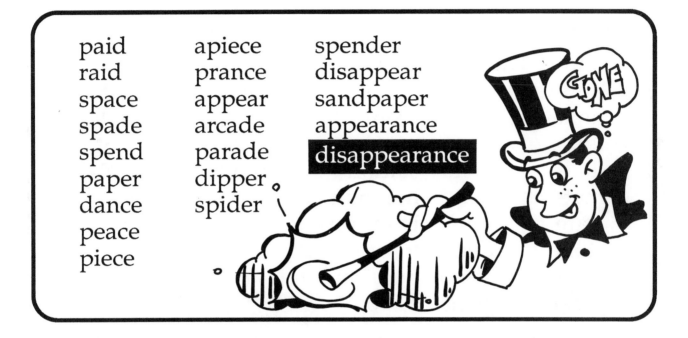

SORT FOR: er aid ade ance piece-peace

Help students notice that sometimes *er* at the end of a word signals a person or thing that does something. Point out that *aid* and *ade* have the same pronunciation, and if you are spelling a word with one of these patterns, you have to see if it looks right or check in the dictionary. Point out morphemic relationships including *appear, disappear, appearance, disappearance* and *piece, apiece.*

WRITING AND NEED TO SPELL:

raider (-aid, -er)
France (-ance)

37.

LETTERS:  a e i i o d m n n p p s t t

A two-day lesson or pick and choose some words.
You may want to make all words one day and sort/spell the next day.

WORDS TO MAKE:

one	tennis	imitate	ointment
done	Dennis	patient	optimist
none	impose	dentist	nominate
tone	donate	pianist	dominate
date	nation	station	insomnia
mate	inmate	mention	impatient
state	insane	mansion	disappoint
stone	indent	tension	destination
point	instead	pension	appointment
piano	instant	appoint	**disappointment**

SORT FOR: ist tion sion ment in im ate one

Help students notice that sometimes *ist* at the end of a word signals a person or thing that does something. *Tion* and *sion* often have the same pronunciation, and if you are spelling a word with one of these patterns, you have to see if it looks right or check in the dictionary. Sort out all the *one* words, and then sort into columns representing the two common pronunciations for *one*. Point out morphemic relationships including *sane, insane; patient, impatient; piano, pianist; and disappoint, disappointment*.

WRITING AND NEED TO SPELL:

inflate (in-, -ate)
imitation (-tion)
nomination (-tion)

38.

LETTERS:  a i o d n r s s t w

The / means that the next word can be made just by changing where the letters are. It is important that students learn that spelling requires not only that all the letters be there but that they be in the right places. Cue students when they will use the same letters in a different order to spell a new word.

WORDS TO MAKE:

own	warn	worst
saw/	wart	radio
was	ward/	ratio
war	draw	drown
	said	straw
	town	stairs
	down	**downstairs**
	trio	
	word	

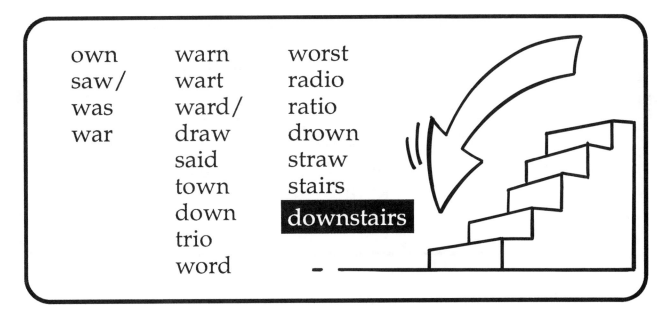

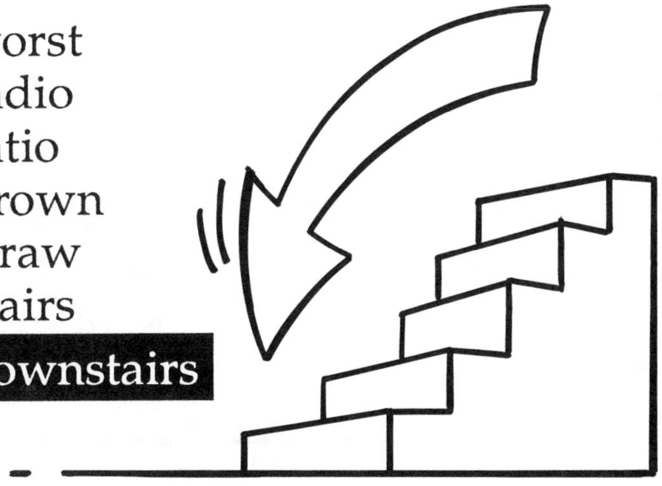

SORT FOR: aw own war-warn, wart, ward
wor-word, worst io-trio, radio, ratio

Help students notice that *own* has two different pronunciations.

WRITING AND NEED TO SPELL:

warm (war-)
reward (-war)

39.

LETTERS:  a a e e u h k q r s t

The / means that the next word can be made just by changing where the letters are. It is important that students learn that spelling requires not only that all the letters be there but that they be in the right places. Cue students when they will use the same letters in a different order to spell a new word.

WORDS TO MAKE:

use
heat
rake
take

shake
quake
quart
earth
reuse

square
Quaker
retake
reheat/
heater
karate
request

earthquakes

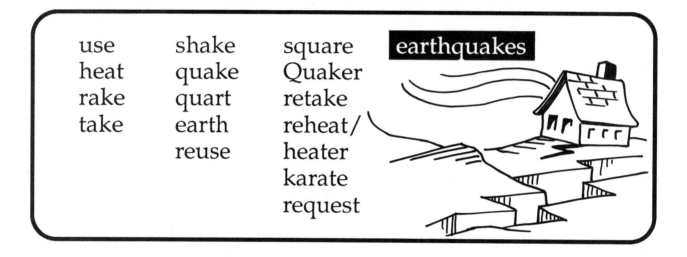

SORT FOR: re qu ake

Help students notice that *re* sometimes means again.

WRITING AND NEED TO SPELL:

snake (-ake)
remake (re-, -ake)

40.

LETTERS:  a e o h m r r s t w

The / means that the next word can be made just by changing where the letters are. It is important that students learn that spelling requires not only that all the letters be there but that they be in the right places. Cue students when they will use the same letters in a different order to spell a new word.

WORDS TO MAKE:

how	earth	warmest
mow	tower/	armrest
row	wrote	**earthworms**
show	horse	
rest	hoarse	
west	shower	
warm	wreath	
worm	warmer	

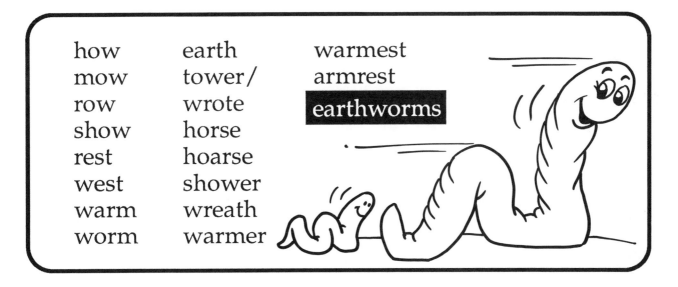

SORT FOR: er/est wr est ow horse/hoarse

Help students notice that *ow* has two different pronunciations.

WRITING AND NEED TO SPELL:

slowest (-ow, -est)
write (wr-)
wreck (wr-)

41.

LETTERS: 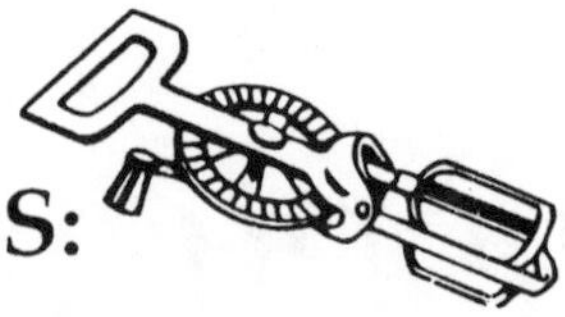 aeeioccdlnpy

WORDS TO MAKE:

ice	cycle	pencil	conceal
icy	candy	police	licence
nice	canoe	policy	cyclone
dice	dance	cancel	cyanide
			encyclopedia

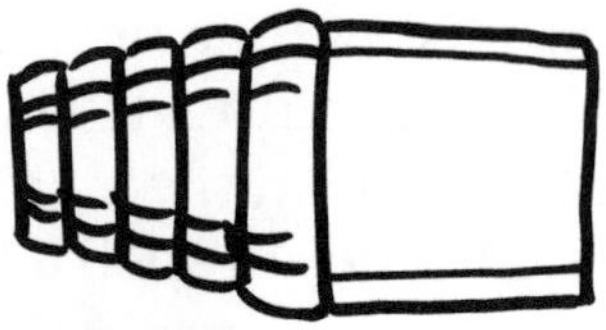

SORT FOR: c ice cy-cycle, cyclone, cyanide, encyclopedia, policy

Help students notice that *ice* and *cy* have two different pronunciations.

WRITING AND NEED TO SPELL:

bicycle (-cy)
twice (-ice)

42.

LETTERS:  aeeeimnnnrttt

WORDS TO MAKE:

eat/	treat	treatment
ate	enter	terminate
rate	inmate	entertain
mate/	marine	entertainment
meat	termite	
neat	matinee	
	nineteen	

SORT FOR: ment ate eat

Point out the *eat-ate* relationship and other morphemic relationships including *mate, inmate; treat, treatment;* and *entertain, entertainment.*

WRITING AND NEED TO SPELL:

repeat (-eat)
statement (-ate, -ment)

43.

LETTERS:  e e i g h n r t v y

WORDS TO MAKE:

Tell students which *there-their* you want them to make before asking them to make these words.

ten	event	entire
hen	every	energy
give	night	thrive
hive	right	either
very	there	neither
ever	their	everything
even	never	
	entry	

SORT FOR: en ive ight there-their

Help students notice that *ive* has two different pronunciations. Point out the *either/neither, ever/never* relationship.

WRITING AND NEED TO SPELL: drive (-ive) enlighten (en-, -ight)

44.

LETTERS:  e e e i m n p r s t x

WORDS TO MAKE:

six	enter	expense
mix	exist	extreme
sent	expert	preteen
teen	expire	present
tire	entire	preexist
exit	empire	experiments
	premix	

SORT FOR: ex pre ire ix

Help students notice that *present* has two different pronunciations and meanings. Point out that sometimes *pre* means before.

WRITING AND NEED TO SPELL: inspire (-ire) require (-ire)

45.

LETTERS:  eioolnpssx

WORDS TO MAKE:

oil	spoon/	poison
soil/	snoop	lesson
silo	spool	lioness
solo	polio	**explosions**
polo/	noise	
loop/	spoil	
pool		
lion		
soon		

SORT FOR: oon oop ool oil lion-lioness

WRITING AND NEED TO SPELL: scoop (-oop) broil (-oil)

46.

LETTERS:  eeionprsssx

WORDS TO MAKE:

ripe	press	express
sore/	siren	snipers
rose	senior	session
nose	prison	soreness
pose	expire	pioneers
snipe	expose	**expressions**

SORT FOR: sion ex ipe ose

Point out morphemic relationships in *sore, soreness; snipe, snipers; press, express, expressions.*

WRITING AND NEED TO SPELL:

swipe (-ipe)
extension (ex-, -sion)

47.

LETTERS:  a e e i c c f k r r r s

WORDS TO MAKE:

Tell students which *fare-fair* you want them to make before having them make these words.

air	rack	crack
ice	sack	career
ace	sick	fierce
face	fire	carsick
race	care	crackers
rice	rare	**firecrackers**
Rick	fare	
	fair	

SORT FOR: c ack ick ice ace air are fare-fair

WRITING AND NEED TO SPELL: space, spice (-ace, -ice); track, trick (-ack, -ick); stare, stair (-are, -air)

48.

LETTERS: 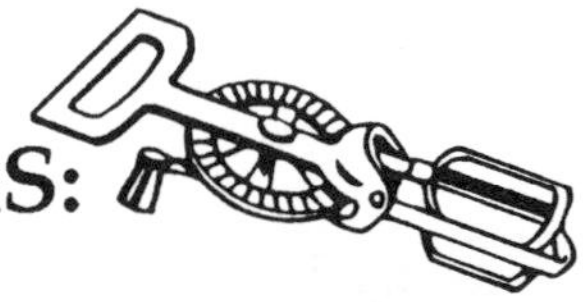 a e o u f l n r t t y

WORDS TO MAKE:

eat	Fran	treat	fortune
not	trot	truly	attorney
rot	tray	neatly	tolerant
lay	true	nearly	fortunate
Ray	fear	tryout	**fortunately**
ran	near		
fan	neat		

SORT FOR: ly ay an eat ear ot

Help students notice the morphemic relationships in the *ly* words and the spelling change when *true* becomes *truly*.

WRITING AND NEED TO SPELL:

yearly (-ear, -ly)
cheat (-eat)

49.

LETTERS:  e i i f g g h n n r t

WORDS TO MAKE:

fire
hire
tire
eight
fight
right
night
hinge

fringe
fright
firing
hiring
tiring
finger

freight
inherit
fighter
fighting
frighten
frightening

SORT FOR: ing ight eight inge

Help students notice the spelling change that occurs when *ing* is added to *fire, hire,* and *tire.* Point out morphemic relationships including *fight, fighter; fright, frighten, frightening.*

WRITING AND NEED TO SPELL:

weight (-eight)
cringing (-inge, -ing)

50.

LETTERS:  a e e i o g n n r s t

Have students make *great* first and then change the letters around to spell the word *grate.*

WORDS TO MAKE:

age
rage
gene
genie
giant
tiger
great/grate
stage
orange
nation
ration
ignore
enrage
entire
engine
ignorant
nitrogen
tangerine
generations

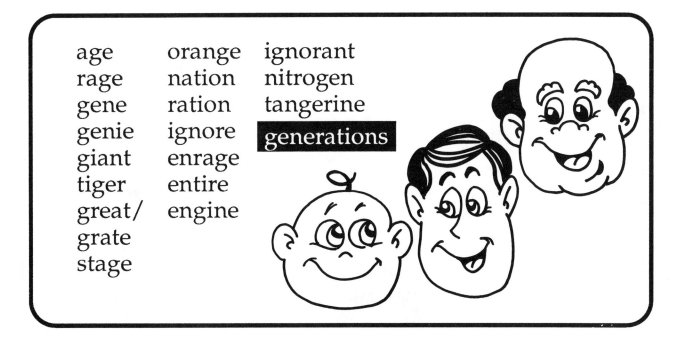

SORT FOR: tion en g (gum/gem) age

Sort the words into columns according to the pronunciation of *g* and then point out that *g* often has the sound of *j* when followed by *i* or *e*. Point out the two pronunciations for *ration.* Help students notice the *rage-enrage* relationship.

WRITING AND NEED TO SPELL:

engage (en-, -age)
mention (-en, -tion)

51.

LETTERS:  e i i d f g l n r r

The / means that the next word can be made just by changing where the letters are. It is important that students learn that spelling requires not only that all the letters be there but that they be in the right places. Cue students when they will use the same letters in a different order to spell a new word.

WORDS TO MAKE:

girl	fined	firing
ride	fired	filing
find	filed/	finger
fire	field	linger
file	fiend	friend
fine	grind	infield
	glide	grinder
		fielding
		girlfriend

SORT FOR: ed ing ide ind

Help students notice the spelling changes that occur when *ed* and *ing* are added to *fine, fire,* and *file.*

WRITING AND NEED TO SPELL:

sliding (-ide, -ing)
blinding (-ind, -ing)

52.

LETTERS:  a a i o u d g n r t

WORDS TO MAKE:

go	ruin	ration
ago	tuna	outran
out	again	aground
dug	round	adoring
rug	around	radiant
ran	ground	duration
run	guitar	graduation
	during	

SORT FOR: tion a-ago, again, around, aground ug

WRITING AND NEED TO SPELL:

thug (-ug)
motion (-tion)

53.

LETTERS:  a e o d g h m n r r t

Tell students which *road-rode* and *Rome-roam* they are making before they make each word.

WORDS TO MAKE:

arm	groan	hanger	mother
road	grand	danger	another
rode	armed	manger	**grandmother**
Rome	other	ranger	
roam	anger	magnet	
moan		dragon	
		moaned	

SORT FOR: ed other anger road-rode Rome-roam

Help students notice that *anger* has two different pronunciations.

WRITING AND NEED TO SPELL:

brother (-other)
smothered (-other, -ed)

54.

LETTERS:  a e o g h p p r r s s

The / means that the next word can be made just by changing where the letters are. It is important that students learn that spelling requires not only that all the letters be there but that they be in the right places. Cue them when they will use the same letters in a different order to spell a new word.

WORDS TO MAKE:

pop
hop
hops/
shop
hero
grass
graph

press
phase
phrase
gopher
proper
prosper

oppress
perhaps
progress
grasshopper

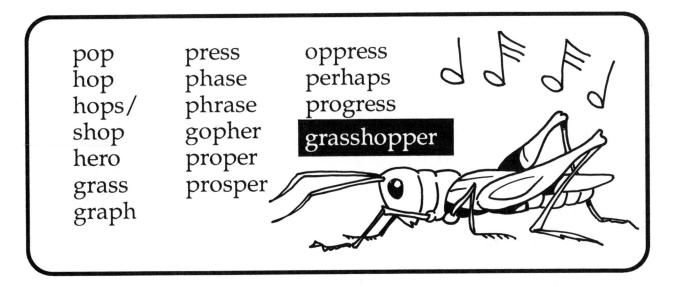

SORT FOR: pro ph ess op

Help students notice that *progress* has two different pronunciations.

WRITING AND NEED TO SPELL:

recess (-ess)
process (pro-, -ess)

55.

LETTERS:  a e u b g h m r r s

The / means that the next word can be made just by changing where the letters are. It is important that students learn that spelling requires not only that all the letters be there but that they be in the right places. Cue students when they will use the same letters in a different order to spell a new word.

WORDS TO MAKE:

us	huge	brush
as	rage	Amber
gas/	sage	ambush
sag	Mars	hamburgers
rag	bush	
rug	mush	
hug		

SORT FOR: g ag ug age ush (bush, brush)

Help students notice that *g* is often pronounced like *j* when followed by *e*. Note the two different pronunciations for *ush*.

WRITING AND NEED TO SPELL:

crush (-ush)
stage (-age)

56.

LETTERS:  a a e e u d h q r r s t

WORDS TO MAKE:

hard	ruder	rudest	headset
head	ahead	square	headrest
rest	squad	harder	treasure
rude	squat	hardest	**headquarters**
	quart	quarter	
	quest	request	

SORT FOR: er/est qu est

WRITING AND NEED TO SPELL:

west (-est)
chest (-est)

57.

LETTERS:  e e i o c h l p r s t

A two-day lesson or pick and choose some words.
You may want to make all words one day and sort/spell the next day.

WORDS TO MAKE:

chop	pitch	heroic	shelter
port	porch	hotels	ostrich
hero	torch	polite	heliport
echo	choir	police	helicopters
itch	cheer	pitcher	
ship	sheer	pitches	
this	shirt	porches	
these	elect	torches	
those	select	reptile	
their	itches	respect	
there/	echoes		
three	heroes		

SORT FOR: s/es ch th sh itch their-there

Have students sort words into *s* and *es* columns and then notice that *es* is added to words that end in *o* or *ch*. Pull out words that share morphemic relationships including *hero, heroes, heroic; pitch, pitches, pitcher; port, heliport, helicopters.*

WRITING AND NEED TO SPELL:

witches (-itch, -es)
switches (-itch, -es)

58.

LETTERS: a i o h l p s s t

The / means that the next word can be made just by changing where the letters are. It is important that students learn that spelling requires not only that all the letters be there but that they be in the right places. Cue students when they will use the same letters in a different order to spell a new word.

WORDS TO MAKE:

sip
hip
hop
hot
hit
sit
spit
spot/
stop
shop
shot
ship
slip
split
pilots/
pistol
polish
hospitals

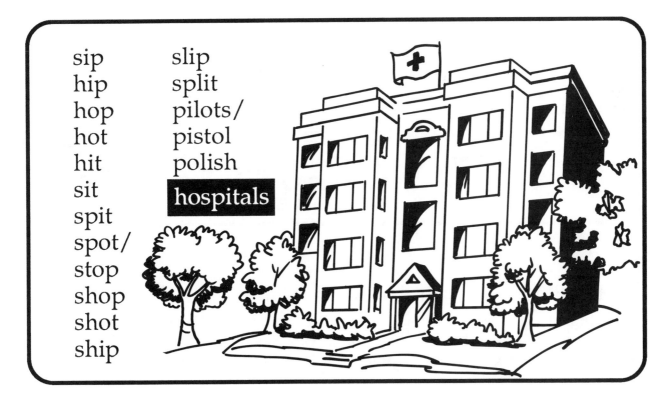

SORT FOR: sh it ot ip op

WRITING AND NEED TO SPELL:

trip (-ip)
quit (-it)

59.

LETTERS:  a e i u c h n r r s

The / means that the next word can be made just by changing where the letters are. It is important that students learn that spelling requires not only that all the letters be there but that they be in the right places. Cue students when they will use the same letters in a different order to spell a new word.

WORDS TO MAKE:

air	racer	nurse
hair	ranch	curse
hare	chair	search
care/	China	rancher
race	share	cashier
cash	scare	hurricanes

SORT FOR: er air are hare-hair

Help students to notice that *air* and *are* are often pronounced the same. When spelling a word, you have to see if it looks right or check a dictionary. Point out all morphemic relationships including *cash, cashier* noting the *i* that is added before the *er*.

WRITING AND NEED TO SPELL :

stare, stair (-are, -air)
fare, fair (-are, -air)

Help students decide what each word means. Check the meanings with a dictionary.

60.

LETTERS:  a a i i i o g m n n t

WORDS TO MAKE:

in	ago	main	again	nation	animation
an	tin	gain	among	ignition	imagination
go	tan		giant	maintain	
	man				

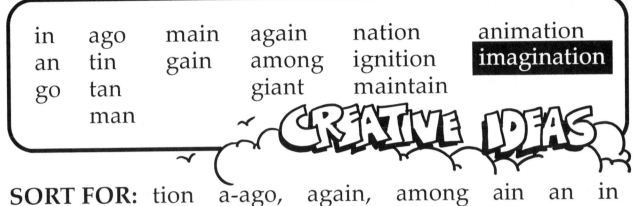

SORT FOR: tion a-ago, again, among ain an in

Write the words *imagine, ignite,* and *animate* on the board and help students notice how spelling changes when the *tion* is added.

WRITING AND NEED TO SPELL:

station (-tion)
sprain (-ain)

61.

LETTERS:  e i i o b l m p s s

WORDS TO MAKE:

imp	soil	bless	mobile	missile	possible
oil	boil	bliss			**impossible**
	limp	blimp			
	mile	smile			
	boss	spoil			
	loss				
	moss				
	miss				
	mess				
	less				

SORT FOR: ile imp iss ess oss oil

Help students notice the three pronunciations for *ile*.

WRITING AND NEED TO SPELL: kiss (-iss) shrimp (-imp)

62.

LETTERS:  e e i i b c d l n r

WORDS TO MAKE:

end	lend	blind	edible	blender	inedible
	dine	blend	binder	decline	credible
	line	diner	lender	recline	**incredible**
	bind	liner			
		cider			

SORT FOR: ible in er ine ind end

Point out that *in* sometimes indicates an opposite relationship. *Er* sometimes indicates the person or thing that does something.

WRITING AND NEED TO SPELL:
intend (in-, -end) incline (in-, -ine)

63.

LETTERS: eeiiubcdlnrstt

A two-day lesson or pick and choose some words.
You may want to make all words one day and sort/spell the next day.

WORDS TO MAKE:

send	cuter	cutest	insider	dentures	incredible
nice	nicer	nicest	include	district	distribute
ride	build	edible	slender	distinct	indestructible
side	dense	direct	builder/	interest	
cute	tense	secure	rebuild	indirect	
	bride	bruise	license	insecure	
		cruise	disturb	inedible	
		sender	dentist	credible	
		tender			
		insure			
		insult			
		inside			

SORT FOR: in ible er/est er ide ense

Help students notice that sometimes *er* at the end of words signals the person or thing that does something. Sometimes *in* signals an opposite relationship. Point out morphemic relationships including *dentist, dentures; build, rebuild, builder.*

WRITING AND NEED TO SPELL:
intense (in-, -ense) incense (in-, -ense)

64.

LETTERS: aiioofmnnrt

WORDS TO MAKE:

in	inn	rant	motor	infant	monitor	formation	information
	fat	into	manor	inform		informant	
	ant	form		motion			
				notion			
				nation			
				ration			
				nonfat			

SORT FOR: in tion or ant in-inn fat-nonfat

Point out the two different pronunciations for *ant*.

WRITING AND NEED TO SPELL: chant (-ant) instant (in-)

65.

LETTERS: eiumnnrsstt

WORDS TO MAKE:

sun	rise	trust	unrest	sunrise	sunniest
set	test	untie	misuse	sunnier	mistrust
tie	rest		sunset		instruments
use	rust				

SORT FOR: un mis er/est ust est
sun/sunnier/sunniest/sunset/sunrise

Point out that *un* and *mis* sometimes signal opposite relationships. Write *sunny* on the board and point out the spelling changes that occur when *er* and *est* are added.

WRITING AND NEED TO SPELL:
mistake (mis-) unjust (un-, -ust)

66.

LETTERS: eiiiomnnrsst

WORDS TO MAKE:

men	item/	inner	insist	monster	emission
ten	emit		insert	tension	minister
			intern	mission	sinister
			sister		remission
					intermission

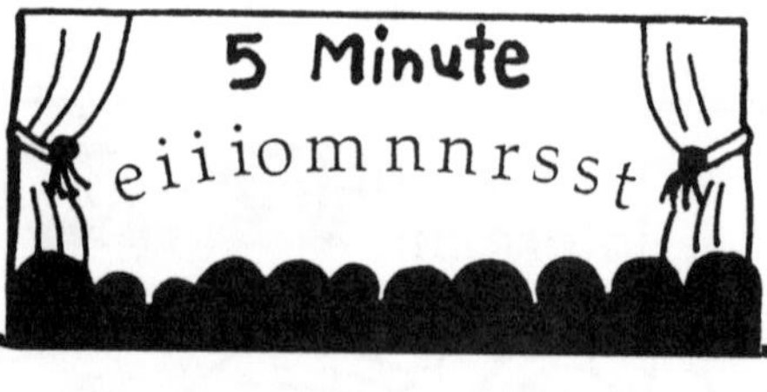

SORT FOR: sion in en

WRITING AND NEED TO SPELL:
then (-en) pension (-en, -sion)

67.

LETTERS: aaeiiolnnnrtt

WORDS TO MAKE:

toe	rent	alien	nation	toenail	national	intention	alienation
air	line	alter	intent	airline	internal		alteration
	nail		rental				intentional
							international

SORT FOR: inter tion al ent

WRITING AND NEED TO SPELL:

final (-al)
mental (-ent, -al)

68.

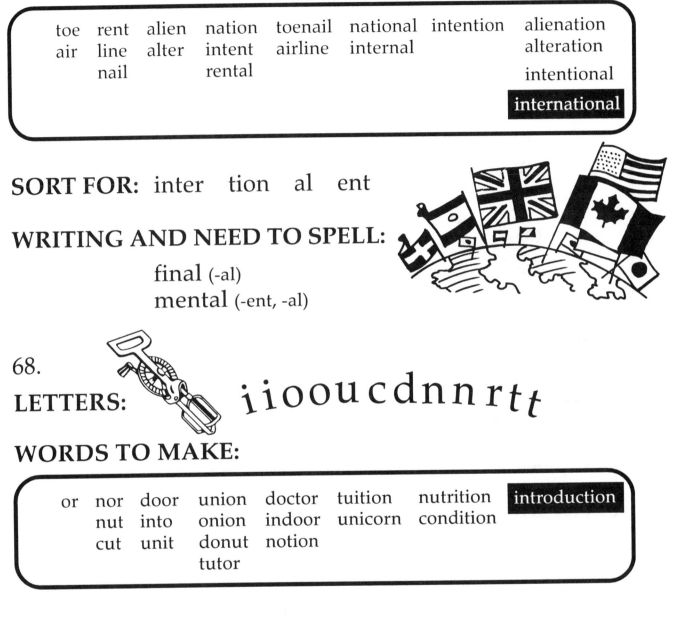

LETTERS: iioouc dnnrtt

WORDS TO MAKE:

or	nor	door	union	doctor	tuition	nutrition	**introduction**
	nut	into	onion	indoor	unicorn	condition	
	cut	unit	donut	notion			
			tutor				

SORT FOR: tion or uni ut

Help students to see that *uni* sometimes means one.

WRITING AND NEED TO SPELL:

strut (-ut)
uniform (uni-)

69.

LETTERS:  a e i i o g n r s t t v

A two-day lesson or pick and choose some words.
You may want to make all words one day and sort/spell the next day.

WORDS TO MAKE:

art	rage	noise	invest	tiniest	investor
rot	test	organ	artist	version	revision
sit	nose	visit	sitter	evasion	organist
age		stage	nosier	visitor	toasting
		store	rotate	senator	rotating
		toast	vision	toaster	rainiest
		taste	tinier	storage	angriest
				noisier	investigator
				tastier	
				tasting	
				testing	
				rotting	
				sitting	

SORT FOR: ist sion ing or er er/est age

Help students notice that *ist, or,* and *er* at the end of words sometimes signal a person or thing that does something. Point out the two different pronunciations for *age*.

WRITING AND NEED TO SPELL:

stinger (-ing, -er)
dentist (-ist)

70.

LETTERS:  e e i i o b l n p r r s s

Tell students which *lessen, lesson* to make before having them make these words.

WORDS TO MAKE:

oil	less	ripen	lessen	pioneer	prisoner	responsible
	bone	risen	lesson		sensible	irresponsible
	rise	bless	person		possible	
	ripe	sense	prison		ripeness	
					oiliness	
					boneless	
					response	

SORT FOR: ible ness en ess lessen-lesson

Point out the morphemic relationships between words including *oil, oiliness; less, lessen; rise, risen; ripe, ripen, ripeness; bone, boneless; sense, sensible; prison, prisoner; response, responsible, irresponsible.*

WRITING AND NEED TO SPELL: illness (-ness) terrible (-ible)

71.

LETTERS:  e i f h j l l s y

WORDS TO MAKE:

elf	yell	shell	jellyfish
fly	sell	shelf/	
sly	fell	flesh	
shy	fill	jelly	
yes	hill	hilly	
	Jill	silly	
	lily	fishy	
	fish	flies	

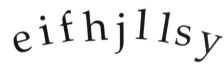

SORT FOR: y ell ill

Sort out all the words that end in *y* and notice the two different pronunciations. Pull out *fish, fishy* and *hill, hilly* and notice the morphemic relationships between these words.

WRITING AND NEED TO SPELL: belly (-ell, -y) dilly (-ill, -y)

72.

LETTERS:  a e e i d g k n n r r t

A two-day lesson or pick and choose some words.
You may want to make all words one day and sort/spell the next day.

WORDS TO MAKE:

ink	rink	knead	intake	earning	endanger
	rank	drink	indent/	trading	gardener
	tank	drank	intend	ranking	kindergarten
	take	taken	taking	earring	
	rage	trade	danger		
	need	enter	darken		
	earn		engine		
	dark		enrage		
	knit		entire		
	knee		garden		
			trader		
			ranked		
			earned		
			earner		

SORT FOR:
ing ed er en(enter-taken) in kn
ank ink drink-drank need-knead

Help students notice morphemic relationships among words, including *earn, earned, earning, earner; take, taken, intake; dark, darken; rage, enrage; danger, endanger; trade, trader, trading; drink, drank.*

WRITING AND NEED TO SPELL:
banker (-ank, -er)
thinker (-ink, -er)

73.

LETTERS:  a a e u g g l n s

WORDS TO MAKE:

sun	glue	lunge	snuggle	language	**languages**
gun	eggs	angel/			
age	guns/	angle			
Sue	snug/				
	sung				
	sang				
	gang				
	lung				

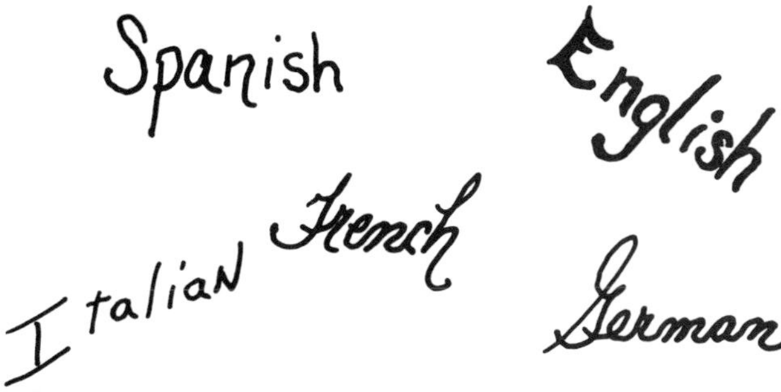

SORT FOR: g (gum/gem) un ue ang ung

Sort the *g* words into two columns and point out the two different sounds.

WRITING AND NEED TO SPELL: stun (-un) untrue (un-, -ue)

74.

LETTERS:  a e e i d h l p r s

WORDS TO MAKE:

red	lead/	plead	spread	dealers/	**leadership**
led	deal	speed	please	leaders	
	dear/	shred			
	read				
	head				
	seed				
	sled				
	sped				
	plea				

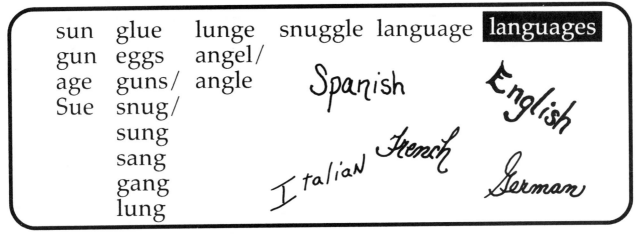

SORT FOR: ed ead eed red-read led-lead

Sort *ead* words into two columns and point out the two pronunciations for *ead*. Point out that *lead* has two different meanings and rhymes with *bead* and *bread*.

WRITING AND NEED TO SPELL: dead, deed (-ead, -eed)

75. 

LETTERS: a e e u c h l n p r

WORDS TO MAKE:

Tell students which *heel-heal* to make before having them make these words.

ace	race	clear	unreal	unclear	leprechaun
	lace	lunch		replace	
	Paul	punch		nuclear	
	haul	uncle		cleanup	
	heel				
	heal				
	real				

SORT FOR: un ace aul unch heal-heel

WRITING AND NEED TO SPELL: crunch (-unch) place (-ace)

76. 

LETTERS: a a o h l l m m r s s w

WORDS TO MAKE:

who/	mall	smash	marshal	marshmallows
how	wall	small		
row	hall	allow		
mow	show	alarm		
low	slow	aroma		
all	Mars	solar		
	rash	worms		
	mash			

SORT FOR: all ash ow

Sort the *ow* words into two columns and note the two pronunciations for *ow*.

WRITING AND NEED TO SPELL:

splash (-ash) snowball (-ow, -all)

77.

LETTERS: aaeuchmsssstt

WORDS TO MAKE:

hut	huts/	teach/	attach	matches	attaches
	shut	cheat	mashes		mustache
	that	chest	cashes		**Massachusetts**
	chat	match			
	math				
	mash				
	cash				
	much				
	such				
	each				

SORT FOR: s/es sh th ch ash

Sort out the *s* and *es* words and point out that *es* is added to words that end in *ch* or *sh*.

WRITING AND NEED TO SPELL:

smashes (-ash, -es) crashes (-ash, -es)

78.

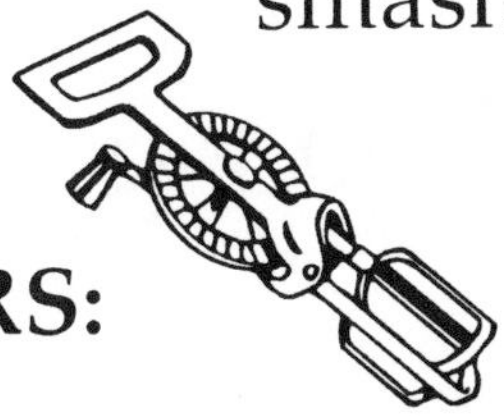

LETTERS: aeeeummnrsst

WORDS TO MAKE:

eat	user/	amuse	nature	steamer	amusement
use	sure	smart	mature	smarten	**measurements**
		steam	assure	measure	
		eater			
		eaten			

SORT FOR: ment sure ture en er

Point out morphemic relationships between words including *eat, eater, eaten; use, user; sure, assure; smart, smarten; steam, steamer; amuse, amusement; measure, measurements.*

WRITING AND NEED TO SPELL:

payment (-ment) capture (-ture)

79.

LETTERS:  eioochmnprs

WORDS TO MAKE:

ice	rich	crimp	chrome	phonics	morphine
imp	echo	chimp	copier	phonier	microphones
		chomp	enrich		
		choir	prince		
		price			
		porch			
		pooch			
		phone			

SORT FOR: c/ch ph imp ice

Sort the words for *c* and *ch* and then point out the two different pronunciations for each. Point out all morphemic relationships including *rich, enrich.*

WRITING AND NEED TO SPELL: shrimp (-imp) twice (-ice)

80.

LETTERS:  eiooccmprss

WORDS TO MAKE:

pro	prom	press	impose	impress	composer
	pose	comic		promise	compress
	rope	scope		process	microscopes
	cope			compose	
	mope				

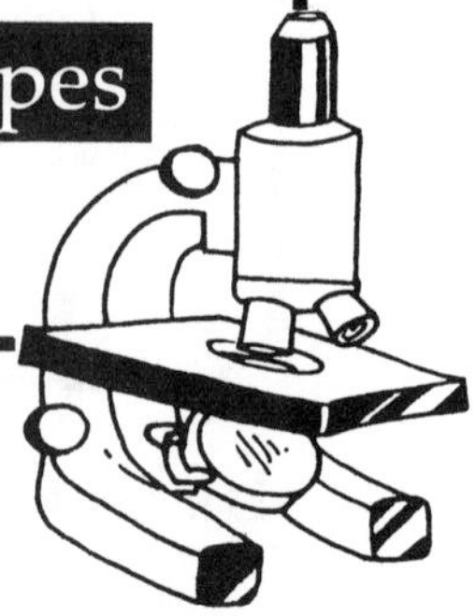

SORT FOR: com im pro ope

Point out the two different pronunciations for *com* and *pro.*

WRITING AND NEED TO SPELL: elope (-ope) combat (com-)

81.

LETTERS: aeiiiollmnr

The / means that the next word can be made just by changing where the letters are. It is important that students learn that spelling requires not only that all the letters be there but that they be in the right places. Cue students when they will use the same letters in a different order to spell a new word. Tell students which *mane, main; loan, lone;* and *miner, minor* to make before asking them to make these words.

WORDS TO MAKE:

name/	alone	remain	airline	millionaire
mane	miner	normal	mineral	
lane	minor		million	
main	lemon/			
rain	melon			
mine				
moan				
loan				
lone				

SORT FOR: ain ane oan one miner-minor main-mane loan-lone

Point out that *ain* and *ane* and *oan* and *one* are often pronounced the same. When spelling a word that rhymes with these, you have to decide which spelling looks right or check in a dictionary.

WRITING AND NEED TO SPELL:

groan (-oan)
plain, plane (-ain, -ane)

Help students decide what each word means. Check the meanings with a dictionary.

82.

LETTERS:  eiiouchmssv

Tell students which *sum, some* to make before asking them to make these words.

WORDS TO MAKE:

use	some	shoes	misuse	mischievous
sum	come	house		
	home	mouse		
	hiss	movie		
	miss	music		
	mess	voice		
	moss			
	muss			

SORT FOR: mis ome ouse some-sum

Point out the two different pronunciations for *ome*.

WRITING AND NEED TO SPELL:

mistake (mis-)
blouse (-ouse)

83.

LETTERS: e o o c c l m r s t y

WORDS TO MAKE:

The / means that the next word can be made just by changing where the letters are. It is important that students learn that spelling requires not only that all the letters be there but that they be in the right places. Cue them when they will use the same letters in a different order to spell a new word.

room	loser	cycler	motorcycles
cost	close	stormy	
sore/	motor	sorely	
rose	storm	costly	
rosy	roomy	looter	
loot	cycle		
lose			

SORT FOR: ly y er ose (rose-lose)

Point out the two common pronunciations for *ose*. Help students notice all morphemic relationships including *room, roomy; cost, costly; sore, sorely; rose, rosy; loot, looter; lose, loser; storm, stormy; cycle, cycler, motorcycles*. Note spelling changes when endings are added.

WRITING AND NEED TO SPELL:

chose (-ose)
closely (-ose, -ly)

84.

LETTERS: a i o u m n n s t

WORDS TO MAKE:

man	main	moist	amount	mansion	mountain
	unit	minus	suntan		**mountains**
	must	stain/	unions/		
	mast	saint	unison		
	mist	mount			
	most				

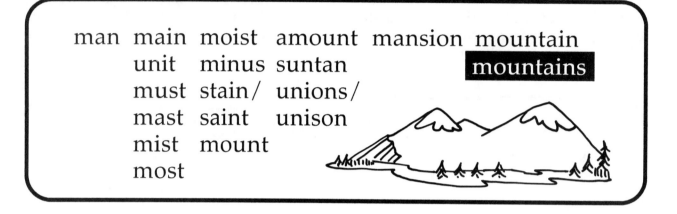

SORT FOR: uni ain ount

Point out the two pronunciations for *ain* and that *uni* often means one or the same.

WRITING AND NEED TO SPELL:

count (-ount)
unicorn (uni-)

85.

LETTERS:  a i i i o u c l l m n p t t

WORDS TO MAKE:

A two-day lesson or pick and choose some words.
You may want to make all words one day and sort/spell the next day.

Tell students which *mall, maul* to make before asking them to make these words.

all	pill	clump	atomic	auction/	mutation	complaint	politician
ill	mill	clamp	amount	caution	complain	municipal	limitation
	mall	count	action	caption		political	multiplication
	maul	mount		tuition			
	Paul	limit		lunatic			
	atom	local		Titanic			
	lamp	total		million			
	lump	panic		capitol			
		attic					
		topic					

2x2=

SORT FOR: tion ic al ill amp ump ount maul-mall

Point out all morphemic relationships including *atom, atomic; complain, complaint; limit, limitation; political, politician.*

WRITING AND NEED TO SPELL:

picnic (-ic)
music, musical (-ic, -al)
gumption (-ump, -tion)

86.

LETTERS: e i o u m r s s t y

WORDS TO MAKE:

try	tour	rusty	stormy	stories	moisture
	mess	messy		serious	mysterious
	rust	moist		tourism	
	rose	tries			
	rosy	story			
		storm			

Point out all morphemic relationships including *try, tries; rust, rusty; rose, rosy; storm, stormy; story, stories; moist, moisture; tour, tourism.*

SORT FOR: ous y-messy y-ies

WRITING AND NEED TO SPELL: curious (-ous) furious (-ous)

87.

LETTERS: e i o o o b d g h h n r s

WORDS TO MAKE:

be	boo	good	shore	bridge	songbird
		hood	snore	booing	neighbor
		bore	booed	boring	neighborhoods
		sore	bored	ignore	
			being/	behind	
			begin		
			brood		
			ridge		

SORT FOR: ed ing ood ore idge

Point out the two common pronunciations for *ood*. Point out all morphemic relationships including *be, being; boo, booed, booing; bore, bored, boring; neighbor, neighborhoods.*

WRITING AND NEED TO SPELL:

mood, wood (-ood) score, scoring (-ore, -ing)

88.

LETTERS:  aeioonprt

The / means that the next word can be made just by changing where the letters are. It is important that students learn that spelling requires not only that all the letters be there but that they be in the right places. Cue them when they will use the same letters in a different order to spell a new word. Tell students which *pane, pain; rain, rein* to make before asking them to make these words.

WORDS TO MAKE:

pane	ratio	option/	portion	operation
pain	patio	potion	painter	
rain	paint		pointer	
rein	point			
riot/				
trio				

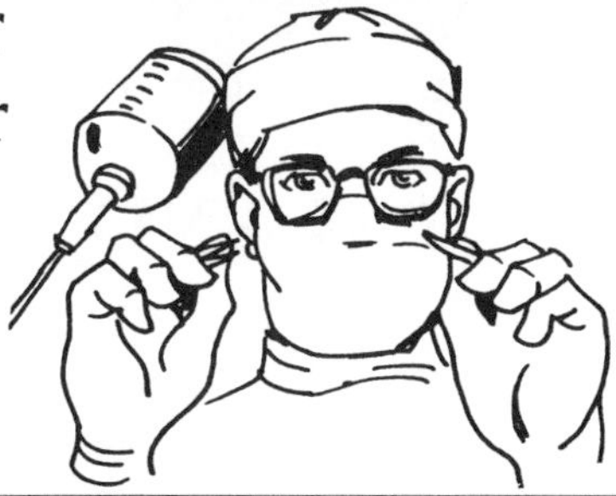

SORT FOR: tion er io-ratio, patio pane-pain rain-rein

Help the students to realize that sometimes the *er* at the end of a word signals a person or thing that does something.

WRITING AND NEED TO SPELL:

radio (-io)
invention (-tion)

89.

LETTERS: aioudgnnstt

WORDS TO MAKE:

do	out	sand	audio	unsaid	distant	astounding
	ant	undo	stand	suntan	instant	outstanding
	and	said	giant	studio		
		soda	donut			
		auto				

SORT FOR: un and ant
io-audio, studio

Help students to notice that sometimes *un* signals an opposite relationship. Point out the two common pronunciations for *ant*.

WRITING AND NEED TO SPELL:
constant (-ant) important (-ant)

90.

LETTERS: aaeuchprst

WORDS TO MAKE:

up	set	hear	spear	search	capture	pushcart
	eat	tear	shear	chutes	pasture	parachutes
		pear	upset			
			earth			

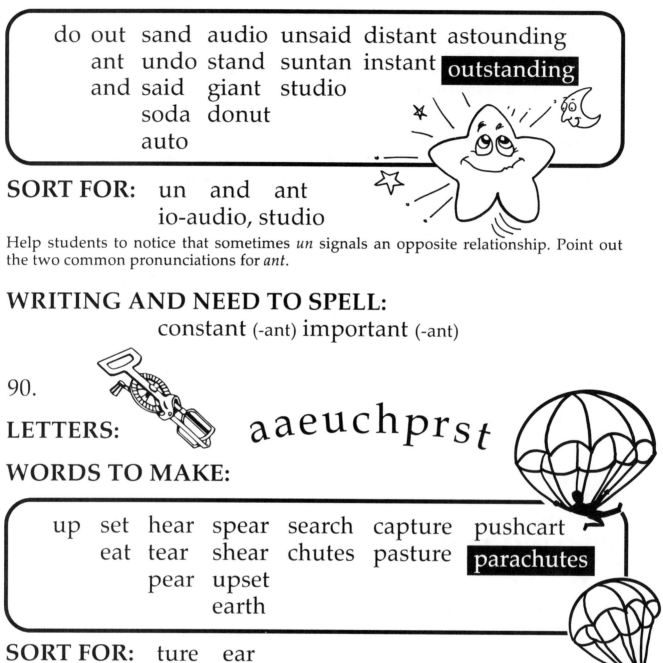

SORT FOR: ture ear

Point out that *ear* has two common pronunciations. *Tear* is actually two different words, depending on which pronunciation is used.

WRITING AND NEED TO SPELL:
mixture (-ture) picture (-ture)

91.

LETTERS: e e c f l p r t y

WORDS TO MAKE:

fee	free	fleet	freely	reflect	**perfectly**
	tree	creep	celery	perfect	
	flee	crept	retype		
	rely	repel			
	left	reply			
	type	lefty			
		elect			

SORT FOR: re ly ee

Point out all morphemic relationships including *free, freely; creep, crept; left, lefty; type, retype; perfect, perfectly*.

WRITING AND NEED TO SPELL: spree (-ee) refill (re-)

92.

LETTERS: a e e o c f m n p r r s

WORDS TO MAKE:

ran	open	fence	reopen	perform	**performances**
cap	face	force	person	enforce	
	once	space	menace	romance	
		peace	prance		
		reran			
		recap			
		refer			

SORT FOR: per re ace ance

Point out all morphemic relationships including *open, reopen; ran, reran; cap, recap; perform, performances*. Note the two common pronunciations for *ance*.

WRITING AND NEED TO SPELL:
chance (-ance) replace (re-, -ace)

93.

LETTERS: eiiomnprss

WORDS TO MAKE:

or	ore	more	ripen	person	impress	emission	impression/
		sore/	risen	prison	mission	imprison	**permission**
		rose	snore	sermon			
		rise	press	impose			
		ripe				OK ✔	

SORT FOR: im sion en ore or-ore

Point out all morphemic relationships including *rise, risen; ripe, ripen; press, impress, impression; prison, imprison.*

WRITING AND NEED TO SPELL:

implore (im-, -ore) expansion (-sion)

94.

LETTERS: aeiolnprsty

WORDS TO MAKE:

real	steal	spinal	spaniel	panelist	**personality**
teal	petal	spiral	apostle	ponytail	
	panel	triple	realist	personal	
	spine	person	parents		
		tinsel	pertain		
		pastel			

SORT FOR: per le/el/al ist eal

Point out that *ist* at the end of a word sometimes indicates a person. *Le, el,* and *al* have similar pronunciations. When spelling one of these words, you have to see if it looks right or check it in a dictionary.

WRITING AND NEED TO SPELL:

persist (per-, -ist) perfect (per-)

95. 

LETTERS: eiocckkppst

WORDS TO MAKE:

pet	kick	spoke	socket	cockpit	**pickpockets**
pit	pick	stick	pocket		
sit	tick	stock	picket		
set	sick				
	sock				
	coke				
	poke				

SORT FOR: ick ock oke et it

WRITING AND NEED TO SPELL:

rocket (-ock, -et) wicket (-ick, -et)

96. 

LETTERS: aoudglnpry

WORDS TO MAKE:

dry	pray	proud	dragon	aground	**playground**
pry	play	young	around	laundry	
pay	ugly	angry	ground		
	your	pound			
	loud	round			
		aloud			
		along			

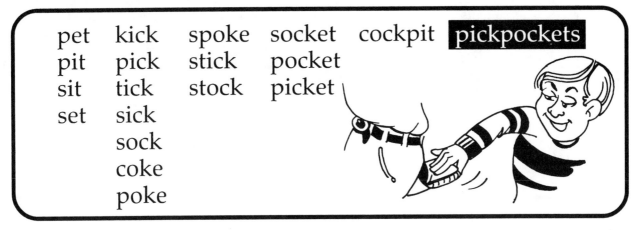

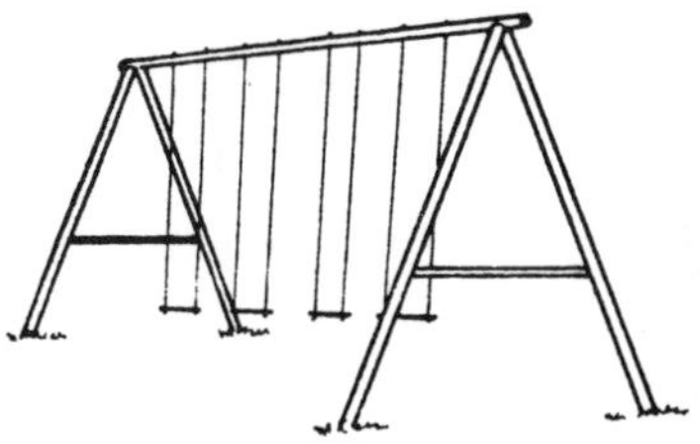

SORT FOR: y a-aloud, along, aground ay
ound oud

Sort out all the words that end in *y* and then point out the two pronunciations.

WRITING AND NEED TO SPELL:

away (a-) cloudy (-oud, -y)

97.

LETTERS: e i o c l p p s s

WORDS TO MAKE:

The / means that the next word can be made just by changing where the letters are. It is important that students learn that spelling requires not only that all the letters be there but that they be in the right places. Cue students when they will use the same letters in a different order to spell a new word.

ice	lips/	close	splice	**Popsicles™**
pop	slip	slice	police	
cop	clip	spice	copies	
sip	slop			
lip	plop			
	pose			

SORT FOR: ip op ice ose

Point out the two pronunciations for *ice* and that *close* is two different words, depending on how the *s* is pronounced.

WRITING AND NEED TO SPELL: twice (-ice) advice (-ice)

98.

LETTERS: a i o o u l n p p t

WORDS TO MAKE:

in	pin	plan	pilot	lotion	optional
	tin	plop	tulip	potion/	**population**
	tan	plot		option	
	pan				
	pot/				
	top				
	pop				
	pit/				
	tip				
	lip				
	lot				
	not				

SORT FOR: tion an in ot ip op

WRITING AND NEED TO SPELL: motion (-tion) promotion (-tion)

99.

LETTERS: eioucnpprs

WORDS TO MAKE:

sun	sure	spine	supper	precious	**porcupines**
son	pure	curse	person		
	cure	purse	prison		
	pine	nurse	copper		
		super	copier		
			cousin		
			insure		

SORT FOR: ine urse ure sun-son

WRITING AND NEED TO SPELL:

vine (-ine) lure (-ure)

100.

LETTERS: eeidnprst

WORDS TO MAKE:

pie	tied/	spent	resent	serpent/	pretends
die	tide			present	resident
tie	rent			pretend	**president**
	dent			preside	
	sent				

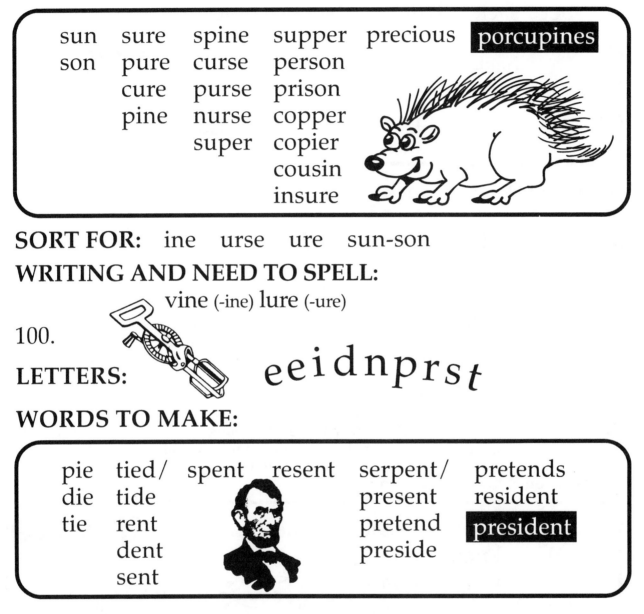

SORT FOR: pre ent ie tied-tide

Point out that *present* has two different pronunciations and two different meanings.

WRITING AND NEED TO SPELL:

prevent (pre-, -ent) prefix (pre-)

101.

LETTERS: a a e u b c k q r r s t

WORDS TO MAKE:

bet	sack	truck	struck	bracket	backrest
set	rack	stuck	bucket	setback	barracks
	back	stack	racket	quarter	**quarterbacks**
	buck	track	basket		
		quack			
		quart			

SORT FOR: qu ack uck et

WRITING AND NEED TO SPELL:
snack (-ack) packet (-ack, -et)

102.

LETTERS: a a e e k l n r s t t

WORDS TO MAKE:

The / means that the next word can be made just by changing where the letters are. It is important that students learn that spelling requires not only that all the letters be there but that they be in the right places. Cue students when they will use the same letters in a different order to spell a new word.

late/	kneel	resale	leanest	anteater	**rattlesnake**
tale	knelt	retest			
sale	later	relate			
lean	snake	rattle			
knee	reset	latest			
		leaner			

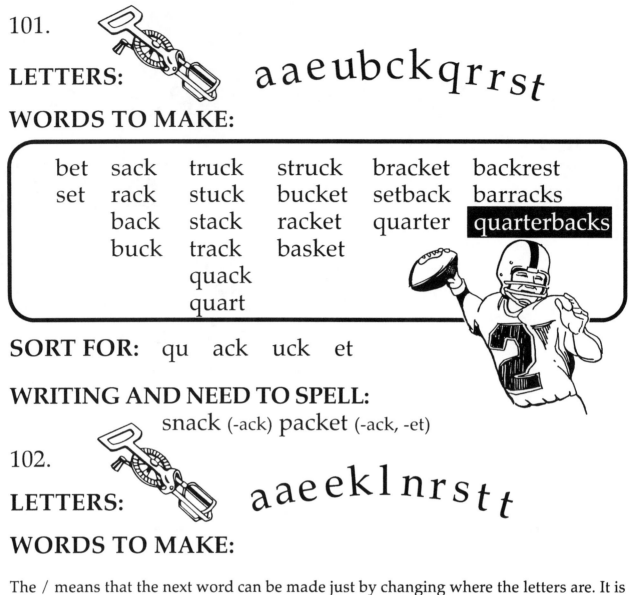

SORT FOR: re er/est kn ale

WRITING AND NEED TO SPELL:
report (re-) knight (kn-)

103.

LETTERS: e i i i o b l n p r s s t y

WORDS TO MAKE:

A two-day lesson or pick and choose some words.
You may want to make all words one day and sort/spell the next day.

try	oily	reply	resist	pointer	pitiless	pointless
spy	only	style	ponies	noisily	oiliness	possibility
oil	less	tries	poetry	stories	possible	**responsibility**
	loss	spies		stepson		
	boss	noise				
	type	noisy				
	poet	bossy				
	pony	story				
	pity	point				
	rely					

SORT FOR: y y-ies re less oss

Point out all morphemic relationships including *oil, oily, oiliness; try, tries; boss, bossy; pony, ponies; poet, poetry; point, pointer, pointless; noise, noisy, noisily; story, stories; pity, pitiless; possible, possibility.*

WRITING AND NEED TO SPELL:

funny, funnies (-y, -ies) helpless (-less) homeless (-less)

104.

LETTERS: e e o u u c f l r r s

WORDS TO MAKE:

use	four	scour	course/	refocus	resource	**resourceful**
our	sour	flour	source	curlers		
for		reuse	useful			
		refer	surfer			
		focus	refuse			

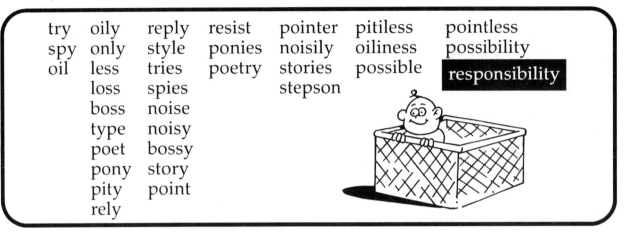

SORT FOR: ful re our for-four

Point out the two common pronunciations for *our*.

WRITING AND NEED TO SPELL:

thankful (-ful) cheerful (-ful)

105.

LETTERS: a a e u n r r s t t

WORDS TO MAKE:

run	true	start	return	stature	saturate
Sue	turn	reran	nature	restart/	restaurant
	rest		statue	starter	

SORT FOR: re ture ue

WRITING AND NEED TO SPELL:

future (-ture) recapture (re-, -ture)

106.

LETTERS: e i o o u l n r t v

WORDS TO MAKE:

lie	vein	unite/	unveil	outline	evolution
tie	veil	untie	oriole	outlive	revolution
	veto	until	revolt		
	unit		lotion		

SORT FOR: un out tion ie

WRITING AND NEED TO SPELL:

unlucky (un-) outside (out-)

107.

LETTERS:  i i o u u c d l r s

WORDS TO MAKE:

rid	sour	solid	curious	ludicrous	ridiculous
lid	soil	scold			
old	sold	scour			
oil	cold	cloud/			
our	slid	could			

SORT FOR: ous id old oud our oil

WRITING AND NEED TO SPELL:
dangerous (-ous) humorous (-ous)

108.

LETTERS:  a e i c d h n s s w

WORDS TO MAKE:

ash	cash	chins	cashes	cashews	sandwich
	wash	ashes	washes	candies	sandwiches
	wish		wishes		
	dish		dishes		
	inch/		inches		
	chin		shines		
			chases		

SORT FOR: s/es ch sh ash ish

Point out that *es* is usually added to words that end in *sh* or *ch*.

WRITING AND NEED TO SPELL:

smashes (-ash, -es) fishes (-ish, -es)

109.

LETTERS: aeeillsstt

WORDS TO MAKE:

it	ate	slit	slate	little	satellites
at	all	tall	still	settle	
	ill	till	stall	estate	
	sit	tell	title		
	lit	sell			
		late			

SORT FOR: le it ate all ell ill

WRITING AND NEED TO SPELL:

squall (-all)
thrill (-ill)

110.

LETTERS: aeecrrsty

WORDS TO MAKE:

are	star	scare	career	secretary
yes	scar	scary	arrest	
cry	east	yeast	artery	
try	easy	tease	secret	
car	care	Terry		

SORT FOR: y ar are east

Notice the two common pronunciations for *are*. Sort out all the words that end in *y* and then notice its two common pronunciations. Point out the *scare, scary* relationship.

WRITING AND NEED TO SPELL:

feast (-east)
square (-are)

111.

LETTERS:  a a e o b d k r s s t

The / means that the next word can be made just by changing where the letters are. It is important that students learn that spelling requires not only that all the letters be there but that they be in the right places. Cue them when they will use the same letters in a different order to spell a new word. Tell students which *break, brake* you want them to make before asking them to make those words.

WORDS TO MAKE:

oak	task	skate	aboard	assorted	skateboards
ask	soak	adore	stroke		
	sore	broke	basket		
	bore	break/			
	tore	brake			
	boss	board			
	toss				
	date				

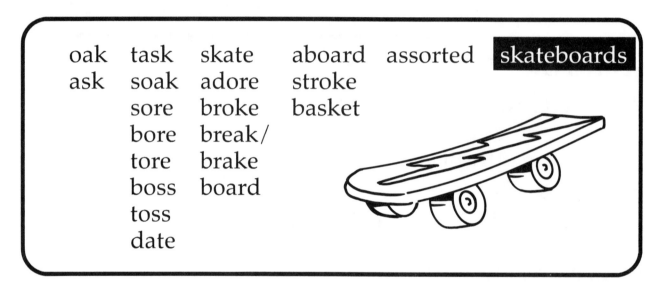

SORT FOR: oke oak oss ore ask brake-break

Help students to notice that *oke* and *oak* are often pronounced the same. When spelling one of these, you have to see if it looks right or use a dictionary. Point out all morphemic relationships including *break, broke; board, aboard, skate, skateboards.*

WRITING AND NEED TO SPELL:

stroke (-oke)
croak (-oak)

112.

LETTERS: a e o f k l n s s w

WORDS TO MAKE:

no	oak	knew	awoke	season	**snowflakes**
	now	know	sneak/	lesson	
	new	snow	snake		
		slow	flake		
		flow			
		soak			
		weak/			
		wake			
		woke			

SORT FOR: ow eak ake oak oke no-know new-knew

Point the two common pronunciations for *ow*. Help students to notice that *oke* and *oak* are often pronounced the same. When spelling one of these, you have to see if it looks right or use a dictionary.

WRITING AND NEED TO SPELL: joke (-oke) spoke (-oke)

113.

LETTERS: a e i g h p s t t

WORDS TO MAKE:

at	ate	seat	stage	**spaghetti**
	age	test	paste	
	Pat	pest	taste	
	hat	past	tight	
	sat	page	sight	
	set		eight	
	pet			

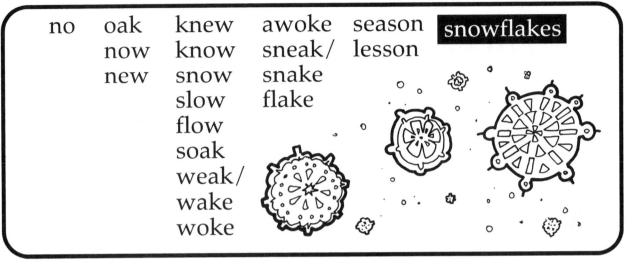

SORT FOR: at et est aste age ight ate-eight

WRITING AND NEED TO SPELL: waste (-aste) flight (-ight)

114.

LETTERS:  a e e i b r r r s s t w

A two-day lesson or pick and choose some words.
You may want to make all the words one day and sort/spell the next day.

WORDS TO MAKE:

was/	rear	waist	eraser	rewrite	waitress
saw	tear	waste	rarest	sweater	strawberries
raw/	wear	stare	wisest	berries	
war	bear/	stair	seesaw		
air	bare	straw	waiter		
ear	rare	sweet	writer		
	seat	sweat			
	beat	swear			
	beet	write			
	wait	wrist			
		wiser			
		rarer			
		erase			

SORT FOR: er er/est wr ear are air eet eat aw
bear-bare stare-stair waist-waste beat-beet

Help students notice that *eet* and *eat* often have the same pronunciations as do *ear, are,* and *air*. Tell them that you have to write the word to see if it looks right or check in a dictionary.

WRITING AND NEED TO SPELL:

meat, meet (-eat, -eet)
hair, hare (-air, -are)
pair, pare, pear (-air, -are, -ear)

Help students use dictionaries to check meanings.

115.

LETTERS: aeiubmnrss

WORDS TO MAKE:

The / means that the next word can be made just by changing where the letters are. It is important that students learn that spelling requires not only that all the letters be there but that they be in the right places. Cue them when they will use the same letters in a different order to spell a new word.

sun	bear/	minus	insure	sunrise	**submarines**
use	bare	rebus	assure	sunbeam	
bus/	sure	amuse	number	marines	
sub	rise	abuse			
	beam				

SORT FOR: sure us use bear-bare

WRITING AND NEED TO SPELL:

confuse (-use) pressure (-sure)

116.

LETTERS: aioubcnrstt

WORDS TO MAKE:

The / means that the next word can be made just by changing where the letters are. It is important that students learn that spelling requires not only that all the letters be there but that they be in the right places. Cue them when they will use the same letters in a different order to spell a new word.

art	burn	toast	carton	auction/	botanist	**subtraction**
	turn	coast	artist	caution	traction	
	tour	boast	action	station		
		bacon		tourist		

SORT FOR: tion ist urn oast

WRITING AND NEED TO SPELL:

lobbyist (-ist) addition (-tion)

117.

LETTERS:  eeeiudnnnprstt

WORDS TO MAKE:

A two-day lesson or pick and choose some words.
You may want to make all words one day and sort/spell the next day.

pin	tied	ripen	endure	striped	stunned	interest	presented
tie	seen	super	entire	preteen		nineteen	president
	teen	enter	pinned	pretend		unpinned	interested
	pest		untied	present		pestered	turpentine
	stun		unseen				uninterested
	deep		deepen				superintendent
	ripe		pester				
			intend				
			stripe				

SORT FOR: en (entire/deepen) un pre ed ipe

WRITING AND NEED TO SPELL:

unkind (un-) enjoy (en-)

118.

LETTERS: eiiouuprssstt

WORDS TO MAKE:

tour	sport	tissue	pursuit	superstitious
rest	press	tiptoe	tourist	
test	issue	stress	serious	
pest		resist	protest	
port		pursue	posture	
sort				

SORT FOR: ess est ort

WRITING AND NEED TO SPELL:

stress (-ess) short (-ort)

119.

LETTERS: eeeohlnpst

WORDS TO MAKE:

he she stop/ slope honest steeple **telephones**

see spot/ elope

pots/ these

post those

host sleep

lost slept

hope tepee

hotel

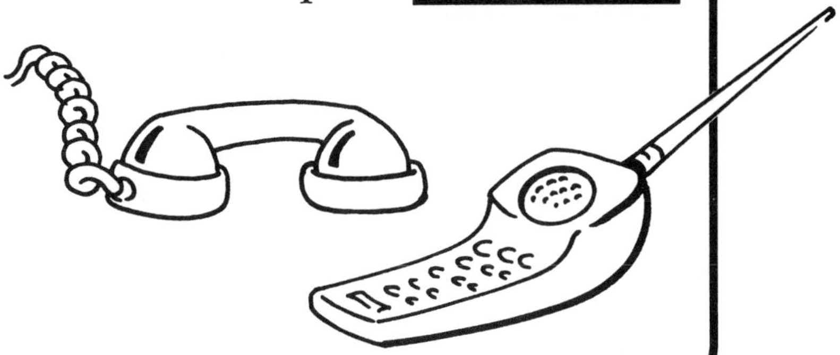

SORT FOR: e ee ope ost

WRITING AND NEED TO SPELL:

scope (-ope) free (-ee)

120.

LETTERS: eeiiolnstv

WORDS TO MAKE:

vest event invite violent novelist novelties

vent novel invest **television**

sent visit vision

vote/ inlet silent/

veto listen

even violin

violet

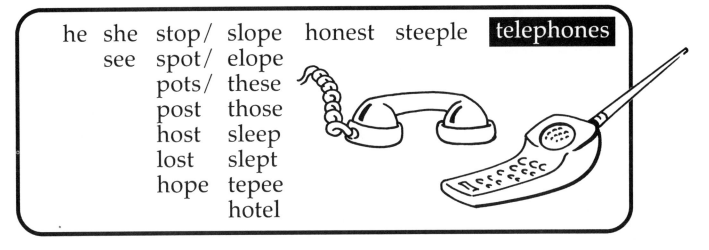

SORT FOR: sion in ent vio-violin, violet, violent

WRITING AND NEED TO SPELL:

indent (in-, -ent) invasion (in-, -sion)

121.

LETTERS:  a e e e u m p r r t t

WORDS TO MAKE:

Tell students which *meat, meet* to make before asking them to make these words.

eat	meat	treat	temper	trumpet	pretreat	trumpeter
	meet	trump	tamper		repeater	premature
			repeat		tamperer	temperature
			mature		mutterer	
			mutter			

SORT FOR: pre ture er eat meat-meet

WRITING AND NEED TO SPELL:

preheat (pre-, -eat) prevent (pre-)

122.

LETTERS:  a i i g g h k n n s t v

WORDS TO MAKE:

ink	sink	thank	knight	sinking	thinking	vanishing
	sing	think	vanish			Thanksgiving
	sang	thing				
	gang	string				
	knit	stink				
		stank				
		sight				
		night				

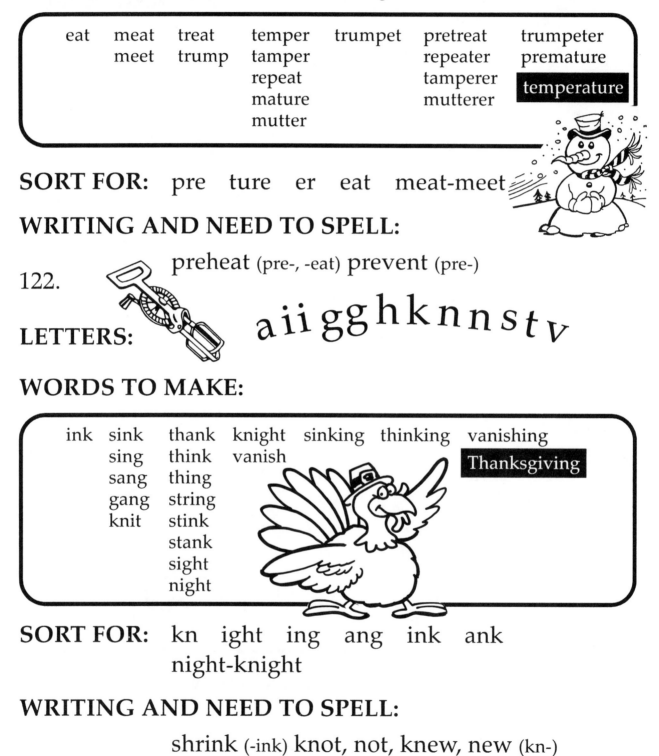

SORT FOR: kn ight ing ang ink ank
night-knight

WRITING AND NEED TO SPELL:

shrink (-ink) knot, not, knew, new (kn-)

123.

LETTERS: e e e o h m m r r s t t

WORDS TO MAKE:

set	them	theme	meteor	mothers/	thermometers
met		teeth	retest	smother/	
		other	remote	thermos	
		reset	mother	restore	
		meter		remorse	

SORT FOR: re th et other/mother/smother

WRITING AND NEED TO SPELL:

brother (-other)
regret (re-, -et)

124.

LETTERS: e o u g h h l s s t t

WORDS TO MAKE:

out	shut/	ghost	outlet	shuttle	thoughtless
hut	huts	guest	outset	gutless	
gut	guts/	guess		thought	
	gust				
	lost				
	host				

SORT FOR: less out ost ut

WRITING AND NEED TO SPELL:

gutless (-ut, -less)
endless (-less)

125. 

LETTERS: eoudhmnrrstt

WORDS TO MAKE:

do	due	true	humor	detour	student	southern
	Sue		tumor	modern	monster	
			rumor		thunder	
			storm			**thunderstorm**
			stern			
			south			
			north			

SORT FOR: ue ern-stern, modern, southern
umor-humor, rumor, tumor do-due

WRITING AND NEED TO SPELL:
northern (-ern) eastern (-ern), western (-ern)

126. 

LETTERS: oo u c d h n s t w

WORDS TO MAKE:

do	too	undo	shown	shutdown	**touchdowns**
to	two/	show	touch		
	tow	snow	outdo		
	cow	town			
	how	down			
	now/				
	own				

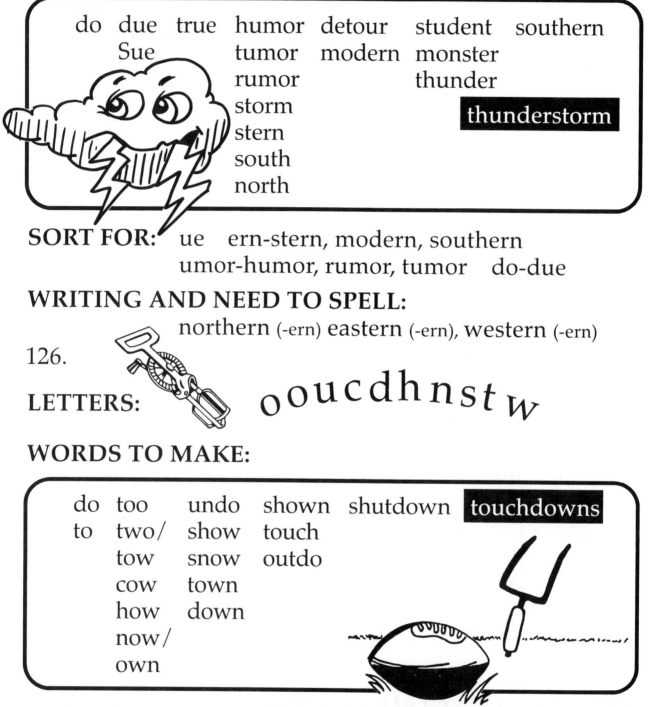

SORT FOR: ow (cow, show) own (down, shown) to-too-two

WRITING AND NEED TO SPELL:
throw, thrown (-ow, -own) flower (-ow)

127.

LETTERS:  a a i o o n n p r r s t t t

WORDS TO MAKE:

pot	stop/	print	sprint	portion	transport
	spot		sprain	station	**transportation**
	pint		strain	patriot	
			potato	airport	
			parrot	nonstop	
			nation		
			notion		
			potion		

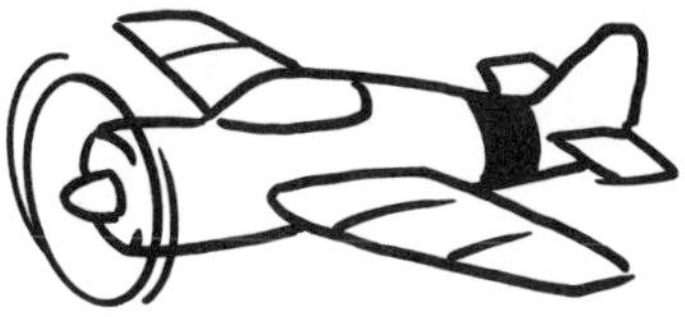

SORT FOR: tion ot int stop-nonstop

WRITING AND NEED TO SPELL: motion (-tion) mention (-tion)

128.

LETTERS:  a e i g l n r t v

WORDS TO MAKE:

Tell students which *tale, tail* to make before asking them to make these words.

rent	trail/	travel	vinegar	triangle	**traveling**
vine	trial	gravel			
tale	rival	rental			
tail	tiger	tangle			
	giant	tingle			
	angle/	native			
	angel				

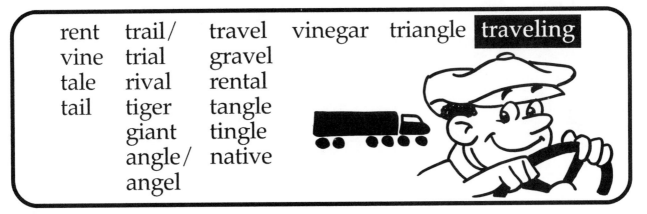

SORT FOR: al/le/el ail tail-tale

Help students to see that *al, le,* and *el* at the ends of words have similar pronunciations. Tell them that you have to write the word to see if it looks right or check your spelling in a dictionary.

WRITING AND NEED TO SPELL:
loyal (-al) model (-el) ankle (-le)

129.

LETTERS:  a e e e i u b b l l n v

WORDS TO MAKE:

The / means that the next word can be made just by changing where the letters are. It is important that students learn that spelling requires not only that all the letters be there but that they be in the right places. Cue them when they will use the same letters in a different order to spell a new word.

be	bee	live/	value	avenue	livable	believable
		veil		unable	believe	unbelievable
		ball		enable		
		bell		eleven		
		bill		unveil		
		bull				
		blue				
		able				

Help students to notice that sometimes *un* signals an opposite relationship.

SORT FOR: un able ue be-bee

WRITING AND NEED TO SPELL:

undue (un-, -ue)
untrue (un-, -ue)

G1499

130. 

LETTERS: a e o o u b c f l m n r t

WORDS TO MAKE:

A two-day lesson or pick and choose some words.
You may want to make all words one day and sort/spell the next day.

arm	tear	crumb	bounce	crumble	comfortable
ran	real	table	unreal	tearful	**uncomfortable**
ear	room	fable	unable	roomful	
	note	clear	outran	careful	
	cure	trace	armful	notable	
	care/	brace	earful	curable	
	race	uncle	tumble	trounce	
	able	ounce		furnace	
	numb			unclear/	
				nuclear	
				outcome	
				comfort	

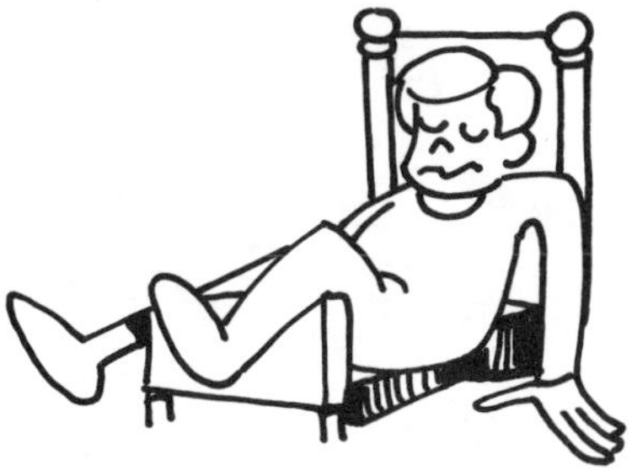

Help students to notice morphemic relationships among words and spelling changes that occur when endings are added.

SORT FOR: able ful out un ace ounce umb

WRITING AND NEED TO SPELL:
painful (-ful) portable (-able) lovable (-able)

131. 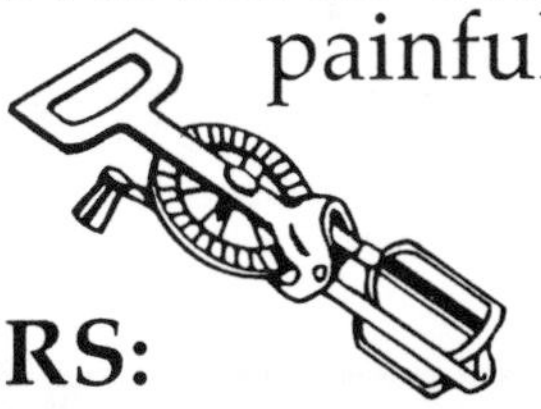

LETTERS: a e e e u b d d l n n p

WORDS TO MAKE:

able	plead	peddle	deplane	unneeded	dependable
bend	bleed	paddle			**undependable**
need	plane	puddle			
deed	pedal	needle			
dead		unable			
bead		unbend			
lead		delude			
		depend			

SORT FOR: un de eed ead pedal-peddle

Help students to notice that *ead* and *eed* are often pronounced the same and that *ead* also has the pronunciation in *dead*.

WRITING AND NEED TO SPELL:
delay (de-) bread, breed (-ead, -eed)

G1499

132.

LETTERS:  e o u u d d g n n r r

WORDS TO MAKE:

go	dog	under	ground	undergo	grounder
	run	dodge	runner	dungeon	grounded
	gun	round	gunner		underdog
			dodger		**underground**

SORT FOR: under er ed ound

WRITING AND NEED TO SPELL:
founder (-ound, -er) underfed (under-, -ed)

133.

LETTERS:  a e e u d k n r r t

WORDS TO MAKE:

run	read	drank	reread	underrate	**undertaker**
eat	dark	drunk	return	undertake	
	take	trunk	retake		
	turn	eaten	darken		
	dunk	taken			
	tank	under			
	rank	rerun			

SORT FOR: under re en unk ank

WRITING AND NEED TO SPELL:
underline (under-) understand (under-)

134. 

LETTERS: a e e o u b f g l n r t t

WORDS TO MAKE:

A two-day lesson or pick and choose some words.
You may want to make all words one day and sort/spell the next day.

for	four	table	outran	enlarge	grateful	fortunate
	real	float	outlet	outrage		turntable
	note	enter	earful	tugboat		unforgettable
	tote	large	bagful	fortune		
	boat	barge	batter	notable		
	goat		fatter	tearful		
	rage		butter			
	able		gutter			
			better			
			letter			
			forget			
			unreal			
			unable			
			enable			
			enrage			

SORT FOR: un en ful able out oat ote atter etter utter for-four

Help students to notice that *oat* and *ote* often have the same pronunciation. You have to write the word to see if it looks right or check its spelling in a dictionary.

WRITING AND NEED TO SPELL: outlet (out-) unfortunate (un-)

135. 

LETTERS: e i u d f l n n r y

WORDS TO MAKE:

fun	duel	funny	dinner	friendly	unfriendly
due	fuel	field	friend		
	rude	yield	rudely		
	rule	rifle	refund		
	fund	under			

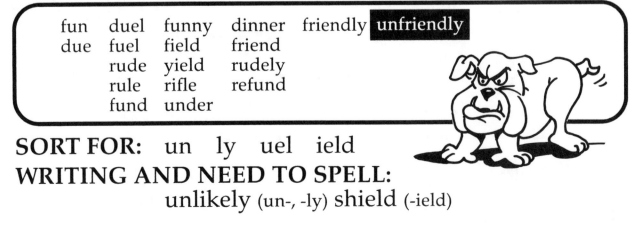

SORT FOR: un ly uel ield

WRITING AND NEED TO SPELL:
unlikely (un-, -ly) shield (-ield)

136.

LETTERS: a e e i l n n s t v

WORDS TO MAKE:

tail	slave	invent	enslave	**valentines**
tale	event	invest	intense	
sale	tense	insane		
sail		tennis		
list		listen/		
sane		enlist		
save				

SORT FOR: en in ail ale sail-sale tail-tale

Help students notice that *ail* and *ale* often have the same pronunciations. You have to write the word to see if it looks right or check in a dictionary.

WRITING AND NEED TO SPELL:
mail, male (-ail, -ale) pail, pale(-ail, -ale)

137.

LETTERS: a e e e b g l s t v

WORDS TO MAKE:

ate	gate	table	sleeve	elevate	**vegetables**
	late	beast	tables/		
	last	least	stable		
	vast	blast			
	east	steal			
	able	steel			
		geese			

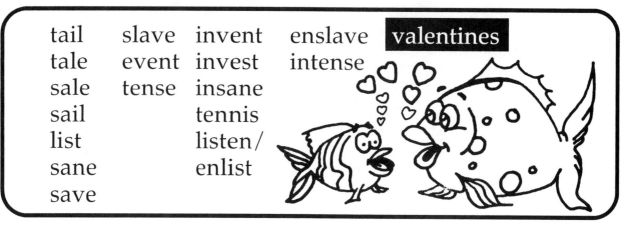

SORT FOR: ate ast east able steal-steel

Point out the two common pronunciations for *able*.

WRITING AND NEED TO SPELL: state (-ate), cable(-able)

138. 

LETTERS: a e e i o d p s t v

WORDS TO MAKE:

see	tape	paste	teased	pivoted	**videotapes**
sea	vote/	paved	vetoes		
tea	veto	voted			
tee	pave	video			
tap	save	pivot			
	past	tease			

SORT FOR: ed ave tea/tee sea-see

WRITING AND NEED TO SPELL:
gave (-ave) shaved (-ave, -ed)

139. 

LETTERS: a e e o l m n r t w

WORDS TO MAKE:

man	mart	water	mental	renewal
men	wart	woman	normal	eternal
war	warm	women		**watermelon**
arm	warn	renew		
art		lemon/		
		melon		
		metal		

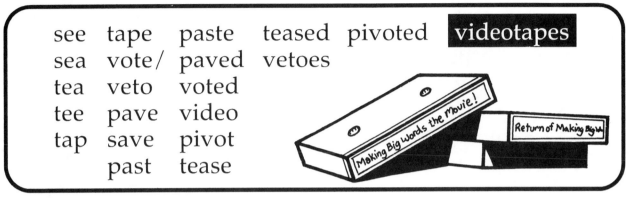

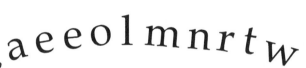

SORT FOR: al art war-wart, warm, warn
man/men/woman/women

Help students to notice the pronunciation of *war* in *war, wart, warm,* and *warn.*

WRITING AND NEED TO SPELL: ward (war-) smart (-art)

140.

LETTERS:  aioghnnstw

WORDS TO MAKE:

Nat	wash	swing	owning	washing	Washington
how	want	wagon		wanting	
now/	show			showing	
own	snow			snowing	
	gnat				
	gnaw				
	wing				

SORT FOR: gn ing ow Nat-gnat

Point out the two common pronunciations for *ow*.

WRITING AND NEED TO SPELL:

bringing (-ing) growing (-ow, -ing)

141.

LETTERS:  eeeighlnssstw

WORDS TO MAKE:

hit	sense	sleigh	wetness	whiteness	weightless
win	sweet	weight	winless	lightness	
wet	sight		witness	sweetness	
	light		hitless	sightless	
	weigh			senseless	

weightlessness

SORT FOR: ness less ight

WRITING AND NEED TO SPELL:

brightness (-ight, -ness) goodness (-ness)

142.

LETTERS:  e i i g h n p r s w

WORDS TO MAKE:

wish	wring	perish	wishing	perishing
ring	gripe	wiping	griping	
rise	swipe	wiring	swiping	
wise		hiring	inspire	
wipe			whisper	
wire				
hire				
wren				

whispering

SORT FOR: ing wr ire ipe ise ring-wring

WRITING AND NEED TO SPELL:

rap, wrap (wr-) rapping, wrapping (-ing)

143.

LETTERS:  e o u d f l n r w

WORDS TO MAKE:

do	dew	flew	under	folder	founder	flounder
	few	drew	owner	unfold		
	own	fold	found	wonder		
		undo				

wonderful

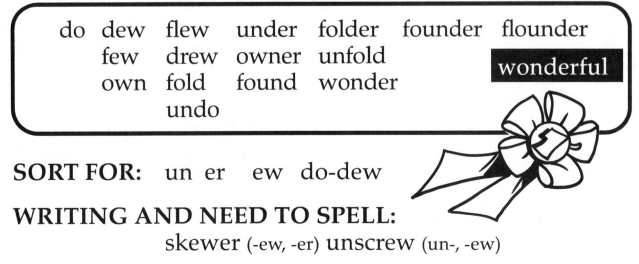

SORT FOR: un er ew do-dew

WRITING AND NEED TO SPELL:

skewer (-ew, -er) unscrew (un-, -ew)

144.

LETTERS: e e o o c d k p r s w

WORDS TO MAKE:

row	word	crowd	powder	crooked	woodpeckers
cow	work	crook			
pow	rock	droop			
	sock	scoop			
	cook	swoop			
	coop	spook			
	cork	worse			
	pork	power			
	crow				

SORT FOR: oop ow ock ook ork
wor-word, work, worse

WRITING AND NEED TO SPELL:
worth (wor-) clockwork (-ock, wor-)

145.

LETTERS: e i g l n r s t w

WORDS TO MAKE:

new	news	wrist	string	glisten	sterling
	grew	write	single	stinger	wrestling
	stew	sling	winter		
	slew	swing	listen		
	wing	sting			
	wren				

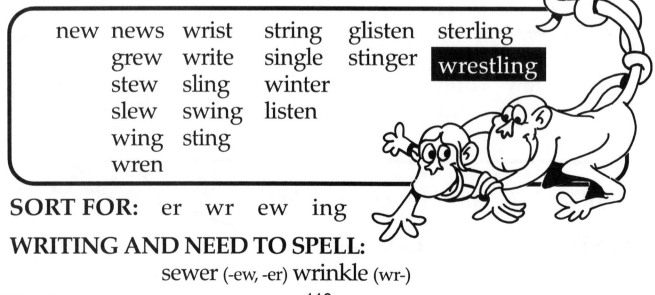

SORT FOR: er wr ew ing

WRITING AND NEED TO SPELL:
sewer (-ew, -er) wrinkle (wr-)

MAKING BIG WORDS
Index of Patterns

Prefixes/Suffixes/Endings

a (ago/again)	apartments graduation imagination playground
able (table/livable)	alphabetical unbelievable uncomfortable unforgettable vegetables
ad	advertisement disagreements
al (spinal/petal)	alphabetical claustrophobia comfortable commercials international multiplication personality traveling watermelon
co (coauthor)	claustrophobia
com	comfortable commercials communities democratic microscopes
con	conservation construction continents convertible
de	advertisement disagreements undependable
dis	advertisement disagreements
ed	girlfriend grandmother kindergarten neighborhoods superintendent underground videotapes
el (panel)	alphabetical comfortable commercials personality traveling
en (eaten/smarten)	advertisement brightness irresponsible kindergarten measurements permission superintendent undertaker
en (enrage/entire)	everything generations kindergarten superintendent unforgettable valentines
er (painter/sister)	breakfast disappearance hurricanes incredible indestructible investigator kindergarten measurements motorcycles operations strawberries temperature underground wonderful wrestling
er/est	advertisement earthworms headquarters indestructible instruments investigator rattlesnake strawberries
ex (extra/expose)	experiments expressions
ful	resourceful uncomfortable unforgettable
ible	incredible indestructible irresponsible
ic (critic)	circulation claustrophobia democratic multiplication
im	disappointment microscopes permission
in (insane/inlet)	advertisement communities disappointment incredible indestructible information intermission kindergarten television valentines
ing	frightening girlfriend investigator kindergarten neighborhoods Washington whispering
inter	international
ist (realist)	advertisement disappointment investigator personality subtraction
le (little)	alphabetical comfortable commercials personality satellites traveling
less	responsibility thoughtless weightlessness
ly (nicely)	fortunately motorcycles perfectly unfriendly
ment	disagreements disappointment entertainment measurements
mis	advertisement instruments mischievous
ness	brightness disagreements irresponsible weightlessness
or (inspector/motor)	conservation information introduction investigator
ous	mysterious ridiculous

out (outlive)	revolution thoughtless uncomfortable unforgettable
per	performances personality
pre (preteen/predict)	atmosphere experiments president superintendent temperature
pro (program/process)	grasshopper microscopes
re	atmosphere celebration convertible earthquakes perfectly performances rattlesnake responsibility resourceful restaurant thermometers undertaker
s/es	chocolates communities helicopters Massachusetts sandwiches
sion	conservation disappointment expressions intermission investigator permission television
sub	claustrophobia
sure	measurements submarines
tion	celebration circulation conservation constitution dictionary disappointment generations graduation imagination information international introduction multiplication operations population revolution subtraction transportation
ture	adventures arguments measurements parachutes restaurant temperature
un	instruments leprechaun outstanding revolution superintendent unbelievable uncomfortable undependable unforgettable unfriendly wonderful
under	underground undertaker
uni	construction introduction mountains
y (fly/fishy/yes)	dictionary jellyfish playground responsibility secretary
y (rain/rainy)	dictionary jellyfish motorcycles mysterious responsibility
y-ies, ier, iest	mysterious responsibility

Digraphs/Consonants

c (cat/city)	celebration chimpanzee convertible encyclopedia firecrackers microphones
ch (chop/machine/echo)	championship chimpanzee chocolates helicopters Massachusetts microphones sandwiches
g (girl/gym)	arguments generations hamburgers languages
gn (gnat)	astonishing Washington
kn (know)	kindergarten rattlesnake Thanksgiving
ph	atmosphere claustrophobia grasshopper microphones
qu	earthquakes headquarters quarterbacks
sh	championship helicopters hospitals Massachusetts sandwiches
th	helicopters Massachusetts thermometers
wr	earthworms strawberries whispering wrestling

Homophones

ate-eight	spaghetti
be-bee	unbelievable
bear-bare	comfortable strawberries submarines
beat-beet	strawberries
break-brake	breakfast skateboards
capital-capitol	claustrophobia
cheap-cheep	chimpanzee
close-clothes	chocolates
deer-dear	adventures
do-dew	wonderful
do-due	thunderstorm
fare-fair	firecrackers
for-four	resourceful unforgettable
great-grate	generation
hare-hair	hurricanes
heal-heel	leprechaun
hear-here	atmosphere
horse-hoarse	earthworms
in-inn	constitution information
led-lead	leadership
lessen-lesson	irresponsible
loan-lone	millionaire
made-maid	democratic
main-mane	millionaire
maul-mall	multiplication
meat-meet	temperature
miner-minor	millionaire
Nat-gnat	Washington
need-knead	kindergarten
new-knew	snowflakes
no-know	snowflakes
or-ore	permission
our-hour	autographs
pail-pale	airplanes
pair-pear	airplanes
pane-pain	airplanes operations
peace-piece	disappearance
pedal-peddle	undependable
plane-plain	airplanes
rain-rein	operations
red-read	leadership
ring-wring	whispering
road-rode	grandmother
roam-Rome	grandmother
sail-sale	airplanes valentines

sea-see	videotapes
sent-cent-scent	continents
stare-stair	strawberries
steak-stake	breakfast
steal-steel	vegetables
sum-some	mischievous
sun-son	constitution porcupines
tail-tale	traveling valentines
tea-tee	videotapes
their-there	everything helicopters
tied-tide	president
to-too-two	touchdowns
waist-waste	strawberries

Phonograms/Spelling Patterns

(* indicates inclusion on the Wylie and Durrell most useful phonogram list)

ace	applesauce chimpanzee comfortable firecrackers leprechaun performances uncomfortable
ack*	crosswalks firecrackers quarterbacks
ade	disappearance
ag	hamburgers
age	generations hamburgers investigator spaghetti
aid	disappearance
ail	airplanes traveling valentines
aim	commercials
ain*	airplanes celebration imagination millionaire mountains operations
air	firecrackers hurricanes strawberries
ake*	breakfast earthquakes snowflakes
ale*	airplanes rattlesnake valentines
all*	basketball marshmallows satellites
ame*	apartments arguments commercials
amp	apartments multiplication
an*	fortunately imagination population
ance	celebration disappearance performances
and	outstanding
ane	airplanes millionaire
ang	astonishing generations languages Thanksgiving
ange	arguments
ank*	kindergarten Thanksgiving undertaker
ant	information outstanding
ap*	alphabetical applesauce atmosphere parachutes
ape	applesauce
ar	circulation secretary
are	firecrackers hurricanes secretary strawberries
art	circulation watermelon

ash*	astonishing championship marshmallows Massachusetts sandwiches
ask	breakfast skateboards
ast	basketball vegetables
aste	spaghetti
at*	adventures astonishing Massachusetts spaghetti
atch	alphabetical chocolates
ate*	advertisement celebration disappointment entertainment satellites vegetables
aul	leprechaun
ause	applesauce
ave	videotapes
aw*	crosswalks downstairs strawberries
ay*	dictionary fortunately playground
e (he)	telephones
each	chimpanzee
ead (bead/bread)	leadership undependable
eak	breakfast snowflakes
eal	personality
eam	apartments
ear (hear/pear)	apartments fortunately parachutes strawberries
east	basketball secretary vegetables
eat*	entertainment fortunately strawberries temperature
ed	boyfriend leadership
ee	perfectly telephones
eed	leadership undependable
eet	strawberries
eight	frightening
ell*	basketball jellyfish satellites
en	everything intermission
end	incredible
ense	indestructible
ent	continents international president television
ess	grasshopper impossible irresponsible superstitious
est*	adventures earthworms headquarters instruments spaghetti superstitious
et	basketball celebration parachutes pickpockets quarterbacks spaghetti thermometers
ew	wonderful wrestling
ice*	celebration conservation encyclopedia firecrackers microphones Popsicles™
ick*	chipmunks firecrackers pickpockets
id	ridiculous
ide*	birdhouse girlfriend indestructible
idge	neighborhoods
ie (tie)	president revolution
ield	unfriendly
ight*	brightness everything frightening spaghetti Thanksgiving weightlessness

ign	disagreements
ile	impossible
ill*	jellyfish multiplication satellites
ime	democratic
imp	impossible microphones
in*	brightness imagination population
inch	championship
ind	incredible girlfriend
ine* (dine/sardine/determine)	advertisement boyfriend disagreements incredible porcupines
ing*	astonishing Thanksgiving Washington wrestling
inge	frightening
ink*	chipmunks kindergarten Thanksgiving
int	transportation
ip*	championship hospitals Popsicle™ population
ipe	superintendent whispering
ire	experiments expressions whispering
ise	whispering
ish	sandwiches
iss	impossible
it*	astonishing hospitals pickpockets satellites
itch	alphabetical helicopters
ive	conservation everything
ix	experiments
oak	skateboards snowflakes
oan	millionaire
oast	subtraction
oat	unforgettable
ock*	crosswalks pickpockets woodpeckers
oil	convertible explosions impossible riciculous
oke*	pickpockets skateboards snowflakes
old	ridiculous
ome	mischievous
ond	boyfriend
one (done/bone)	boyfriend continents disappointment millionaire
ood (good/food)	neighborhoods
ook	woodpeckers
ool	chocolates explosions
oon	conservation constitution explosions
oop	explosions woodpeckers
op*	championship grasshopper hospitals Popsicles™ population
ope	microscope telephones
ore*	neighborhoods permission skateboards

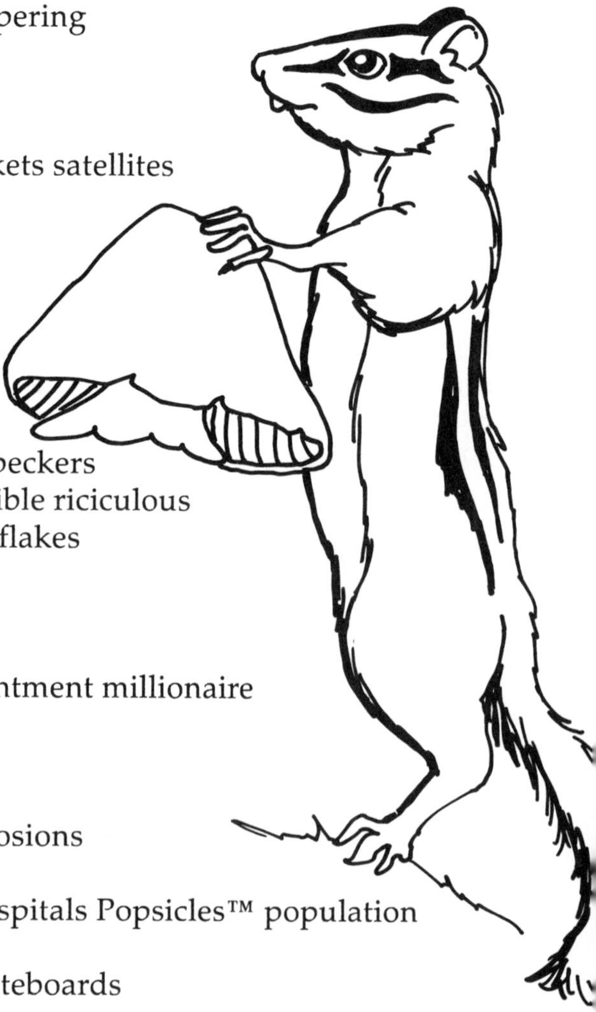

ork	woodpeckers
ort	autographs superstitious
ose	birdhouse expressions motorcycles Popsicles™
oss	impossible responsibility skateboards
ost (cost/host)	claustrophobia computers telephones thoughtless
ot*	fortunately hospitals population transportation
ote	unforgettable
ouch	claustrophobia
oud	playground ridiculous
ough	autographs
ought	autographs
ounce	uncomfortable
ound	playground underground
ount	mountains multiplication
oup	autographs
our (our/four)	resourceful ridiculous
ouse	mischievous
out	constitution construction
ow (how/show)	crosswalks earthworms marshmallows snowflakes touchdowns Washington woodpeckers
own (down/shown)	downstairs touchdowns
ub	birdhouse
uck*	quarterbacks
ue	arguments languages restaurant thunderstorm unbelievable
uel	unfriendly
ug*	arguments autographs graduation hamburgers
umb	uncomfortable
ump*	chipmunks multiplication
un	languages restaurant
unch	chipmunks leprechaun
ung	languages
unk*	chipmunks undertaker
ure	porcupines
urn	subtraction
urse	porcupines
urt	autographs
us	submarines
use	arguments measurements submarines
ush (bush/hush)	birdhouse claustrophobia hamburgers
ust	computers instruments mysterious
ut	introduction Massachusetts thoughtless
ute	communities computers

Compound Words

airline	international
airplanes	airplanes
airport	transportation
another	grandmother
applesauce	applesauce
armrest	earthworms
backrest	quarterbacks
barefoot	comfortable
basketball	basketball
birdhouse	birdhouse
boyfriend	boyfriend
cannot	conservation
cleanup	leprechaun
cockpit	pickpockets
crosswalk	crosswalks
downstairs	downstairs
earlobe	celebration
earring	kindergarten
earthquakes	earthquakes
earthworms	earthworms
everything	everything
footrace	comfortable
girlfriend	girlfriend
grandmother	grandmother
grasshopper	grasshopper
haircut	claustrophobia
headquarters	headquarters
headrest	headquarters
headset	headquarters
income	communities
indoor	introduction
infield	girlfriend
inlet	television
into	communities introduction
jellyfish	jellyfish
motorcycles	motorcycles
outlet	thoughtless
outline	revolution
outlive	revolution
outset	thoughtless
overcast	conservation
pickpockets	pickpockets
playground	playground
ponytail	personality
pushcart	parachutes
quarterbacks	quarterbacks
rattlesnake	rattlesnake

rosebud	birdhouse
sailboat	claustrophobia
sandpaper	disappearance
seesaw	strawberries
setback	quarterbacks
shutdown	touchdowns
skateboards	skateboards
snowflakes	snowflakes
songbird	neighborhoods
strawberries	strawberries
sunbeam	submarines
sunrise	submarines
suntan	mountains outstanding
tiptoe	superstitious
toenail	international
touchdowns	touchdowns
tryout	fortunately
tugboat	unforgettable
turntable	unforgettable
undertaker	undertaker
upset	parachutes
videotapes	videotapes
watermelon	watermelon
woodpeckers	woodpeckers

Dear Parents,

Making Words is an important activity we work on in our class. Making Words is an active, hands-on activity that students learn by doing. Each day as we "make words," your child learns more about letters and letter sounds (phonics). As children manipulate the letters they are given, they have an opportunity to discover more about letter-sound relationships, and as they look for patterns in words, they have an opportunity to see how these letter-sound relationships work in words. These two activities help students read and spell even more words! The children may enjoy these lessons, but more importantly these skills increase their word knowledge which will help them become even better students in the future.

When the students bring home these letter strips, they are asked to cut the letter strips apart into the individual letters. Next, they are asked to see how many words they can make. Finally, they should take some of the words and put them into groups (your child knows what to do). You may want to work together or just see the finished list and how the words were sorted. Working with words can be fun as well as educational!

Sincerely,

Your child's teacher

1. a e e u d n r s t v

2. a e e e i d m n r s t t v

3. a a e i l n p r s

4. a a a e i b c h l l p t

5. a a e m n p r s t t

6. a a e e u c l p p s

7. a e u g m n r s t

8. a i i o g h n n s s t

9. a e e o h m p r s t

10. a a o u g h p r s t

11. a a e b b k l l s t

12. e i o u b d h r s

V T S R N D U E E A 1.

V T T S R N M D I E E E A 2.

S R P N L I E A A 3.

T P L L H C B I E A A A 4.

T T S R P N M E A A 5.

S P P L C U E E A A 6.

T S R N M G U E A 7.

T S S N N H G O I I A 8.

T S R P M H O E E A 9.

T S R P H G U O A A 10.

T S L L K B B E A A 11.

S R H D B U O I E 12.

13. e i o b d f n r y

14. a a e b f k r s t

15. e i b g h n r s s t

16. a e e i o b c l n r t

17. a i i o c h h m n p p s

18. a e e i c h m n p z

19. i u c h k m n p s

20. a e o o c c h l s t

21. a i i o u c c l n r t

22. a a i o o u b c h l p r s t

23. a e o o b c f l m r t

24. a e i o c c l m m r s

Y R N F D B O I E 13.

T S R K F B E A A 14.

T S S R N H G B I E 15.

T R N L C B O I E E A 16.

S P P N M H H C O I I A 17.

Z P N M H C I E E A 18.

S P N M K H C U I 19.

T S L H C C O O E A 20.

T R N L C C U O I I A 21.

T S R P L H C B U O O I A A 22.

T R M L F C B O O E A 23.

S R M M L C C O I E A 24.

25. e i i o u c m m n s t

26. e o u c m p r s t

27. a e i o o c n n r s t v

28. i i o o u c n n s t t t

29. i o o u c c n n r s t t

30. e i o c n n n s t t

31. e e i o b c l n r t v

32. a o c k l r s s s w

33. a e i o c c d m r t

34. a i i o c d n r t y

35. a e e e i d g m n r s s t

36. a a a e e i c d n p p r s

T S N M M C U O I I E 25.

T S R P M C U O E 26.

V T S R N N C O O I E A 27.

T T T S N N C U O O I I 28.

T T S R N N C C U O O I 29.

T T S N N N C O I E 30.

V T R N L C B O I E E 31.

W S S S R L K C O A 32.

T R M D C C O I E A 33.

Y T R N D C O I I A 34.

T S S R N M G D I E E E A 35.

S R P P N D C I E E A A A 36.

37. a e i i o d m n n p p s t t

38. a i o d n r s s t w

39. a a e e u h k q r s t

40. a e o h m r r s t w

41. a e e i o c c d l n p y

42. a e e e i m n n n r t t t

43. e e i g h n r t v y

44. e e e i m n p r s t x

45. e i o o l n p s s x

46. e e i o n p r s s s x

47. a e e i c c f k r r r s

48. a e o u f l n r t t y

T	T	S	P	P	N	N	M	D	O	I	I	E	A	37.
				W	T	S	S	R	N	D	O	I	A	38.
			T	S	R	Q	K	H	U	E	E	A	A	39.
				W	T	S	R	R	M	H	O	E	A	40.
		Y	P	N	L	D	C	C	O	I	E	E	A	41.
	T	T	T	R	N	N	N	M	I	E	E	E	A	42.
				Y	V	T	R	N	H	G	I	E	E	43.
			X	T	S	R	P	N	M	I	E	E	E	44.
				X	S	S	P	N	L	O	O	I	E	45.
			X	S	S	S	R	P	N	O	I	E	E	46.
		S	R	R	R	K	F	C	C	I	E	E	A	47.
			Y	T	T	R	N	L	F	U	O	E	A	48.

49. e i i f g g h n n r t

50. a e e i o g n n r s t

51. e i i d f g l n r r

52. a a i o u d g n r t

53. a e o d g h m n r r t

54. a e o g h p p r r s s

55. a e u b g h m r r s

56. a a e e u d h q r r s t

57. e e i o c h l p r s t

58. a i o h l p s s t

59. a e i u c h n r r s

60. a a i i i o g m n n t

T R N N H G G F I I E 49.

T S R N N G O I E E A 50.

R R N L G F D I I E 51.

T R N G D U O I A A 52.

T R R N M H G D O E A 53.

S S R R P P H G O E A 54.

S R R M H G B U E A 55.

T S R R Q H D U E E A A 56.

T S R P L H C O I E E 57.

T S S P L H O I A 58.

S R R N H C U I E A 59.

T N N M G O I I I A A 60.

61. e i i o b l m p s s

62. e e i i b c d l n r

63. e e i i u b c d l n r s t t

64. a i i o o f m n n r t

65. e i u m n n r s s t t

66. e i i i o m n n r s s t

67. a a e i i o l n n n r t t

68. i i o o u c d n n r t t

69. a e i i o g n r s t t v

70. e e i i o b l n p r r s s

71. e i f h j l l s y

72. a e e i d g k n n r r t

S S P M L B O I I E	61.
R N L D C B I I E E	62.
T T S R N L D C B U I I E E	63.
T R N N M F O O I I A	64.
T T S S R N N M U I E	65.
T S S R N N M O I I I E	66.
T T R N N N L O I I E A A	67.
T T R N N D C U O O I I	68.
V T T S R N G O I I E A	69.
S S R R P N L B O I I E E	70.
Y S L L J H F I E	71.
T R R N N K G D I E E A	72.

73. a a e u g g l n s

74. a e e i d h l p r s

75. a e e u c h l n p r

76. a a o h l l m m r s s w

77. a a e u c h m s s s s t t

78. a e e e u m m n r s s t

79. e i o o c h m n p r s

80. i e o o c c m p r s s

81. a e i i i o l l m n r

82. e i i o u c h m s s v

83. e o o c c l m r s t y

84. a i o u m n n s t

S N L G G U E A A 73.

S R P L H D I E E A 74.

R P N L H C U E E A 75.

W S S R M M L L H O A A 76.

T T S S S S M H C U E A A 77.

T S S R N M M U E E E A 78.

S R P N M H C O O I E 79.

S S R P M C C O O E I 80.

R N M L L O I I I E A 81.

V S S M H C U O I I E 82.

Y T S R M L C C O O E 83.

T S N N M U O I A 84.

85. a i i i o u c l l m n p t t

86. e i o u m r s s t y

87. e i o o o b d g h h n r s

88. a e i o o n p r t

89. a i o u d g n n s t t

90. a a e u c h p r s t

91. e e c f l p r t y

92. a e e o c f m n p r r s

93. e i i o m n p r s s

94. a e i o l n p r s t y

95. e i o c c k k p p s t

96. a o u d g l n p r y

T T P N M L L C U O I I I A 85.

Y T S S R M U O I E 86.

S R N H H G D B O O O I E 87.

T R P N O O I E A 88.

T T S N N G D U O I A 89.

T S R P H C U E A A 90.

Y T R P L F C E E 91.

S R R P N M F C O E E A 92.

S S R P N M O I I E 93.

Y T S R P N L O I E A 94.

T S P P K K C C O I E 95.

Y R P N L G D U O A 96.

97. e i o c l p p s s

98. a i o o u l n p p t

99. e i o u c n p p r s

100. e e i d n p r s t

101. a a e u b c k q r r s t

102. a a e e k l n r s t t

103. e i i i o b l n p r s s t y

104. e e o u u c f l r r s

105. a a e u n r r s t t

106. e i o o u l n r t v

107. i i o u u c d l r s

108. a e i c d h n s s w

S S P P L C O I E 97.

T P P N L U O O I A 98.

S R P P N C U O I E 99.

T S R P N D I E E 100.

T S R R Q K C B U E A A 101.

T T S R N L K E E A A 102.

Y T S S R P N L B O I I I E 103.

S R R L F C U U O E E 104.

T T S R R N U E A A 105.

V T R N L U O O I E 106.

S R L D C U U O I I 107.

W S S N H D C I E A 108.

109. a e e i l l s s t t

110. a e e c r r s t y

111. a a e o b d k r s s t

112. a e o f k l n s s w

113. a e i g h p s t t

114. a e e i b r r r s s t w

115. a e i u b m n r s s

116. a i o u b c n r s t t

117. e e e i u d n n n p r s t t

118. e i i o u u p r s s s t t

119. e e e o h l n p s t

120. e e i i o l n s t v

T T S S L L I E E A 109.

Y T S R R C E E A 110.

T S S R K D B O E A A 111.

W S S N L K F O E A 112.

T T S P H G I E A 113.

W T S S R R R B I E E A 114.

S S R N M B U I E A 115.

T T S R N C B U O I A 116.

T T S R P N N N D U I E E E 117.

T T S S S R P U U O I I E 118.

T S P N L H O E E E 119.

V T S N L O I I E E 120.

121. a e e e u m p r r t t

122. a i i g g h k n n s t v

123. e e e o h m m r r s t t

124. e o u g h h l s s t t

125. e o u d h m n r r s t t

126. o o u c d h n s t w

127. a a i o o n n p r r s t t t

128. a e i g l n r t v

129. a e e e i u b b l l n v

130. a e o o u b c f l m n r t

131. a e e e u b d d l n n p

132. e o u u d d g n n r r

T T R R P M U E E E A 121.

V T S N N K H G G I I A 122.

T T S R R M M H O E E E 123.

T T S S L H H G U O E 124.

T T S R R N M H D U O E 125.

W T S N H D C U O O 126.

T T T S R R P N N O O I A A 127.

V T R N L G I E A 128.

V N L L B B U I E E E A 129.

T R N M L F C B U O O E A 130.

P N N L D D B U E E E A 131.

R R N N G D D U U O E 132.

133. a e e u d k n r r t

134. a e e o u b f g l n r t t

135. e i u d f l n n r y

136. a e e i l n n s t v

137. a e e e b g l s t v

138. a e e i o d p s t v

139. a e e o l m n r t w

140. a i o g h n n s t w

141. e e e i g h l n s s s s t w

142. e i i g h n p r s w

143. e o u d f l n r w

144. e e o o c d k p r s w

T R R N K D U E E A 133.

T T R N L G F B U O E E A 134.

Y R N N L F D U I E 135.

V T S N N L I E E A 136.

V T S L G B E E E A 137.

V T S P D O I E E A 138.

W T R N M L O E E A 139.

W T S N N H G O I A 140.

W T S S S S N L H G I E E E 141.

W S R P N H G I I E 142.

W R N L F D U O E 143.

W S R P K D C O O E E 144.

145. e i g l n r s t w

145. E I G L N R S T W